*From Accidents to Zero: A Practical Guide t...* traditional safety and health books. Sharman ... "business as usual" if we want to approach zero h... organizations tend to have difficulties in continuin... see our own limitations and "blindness" in our saf... immediate action!
**Professor Dr Jukka Takala, Director Emeritus, ILO Safework & EU-OSHA.**
**Ministry of Manpower Services Centre, Workplace Safety & Health Institute, Singapore**

*Thought-provoking and insightful.* From Accidents to Zero *progressively pushed me to see new connections, and new ways to address organizations' safety culture and risk management challenges.*
**Mieke Jacobs, Global Practice Leader – Employee Safety, DuPont**

*This is a must read – this book will change your approach to safety forever! Challenges your everyday thinking and provides innovative and proactive methods to truly integrate and embed safety into your company culture.*
**Steve Bourke, EHS Director, Owens-Illinois**

*This book should be subtitled 'safety psychology without tears'. If you want to know more about what makes people behave as they do and how you can translate that knowledge into smarter worker protection, Sharman's your man.*
**Louis Wustemann, Managing Editor, Health & Safety at Work magazine**

*A pithy, punchy, provoking publication.*
**Gerard Forlin QC, Cornerstone Barristers – London, Denman Chambers – Sydney, Maxwell Chambers – Singapore & Vice Chair, Health and Safety Lawyers Association**

*Take a time-out from the power-point factory today and remind yourself how you can save lives, stop injuries and unlock the potential of your teams to drive a culture shift with this fresh and direct step-by-step user guide.*
**Peter McLellan, Global Head of Health & Safety, DHL**

*The UK's health and safety legacy is arguably second to none. Yet, while the track record in slashing fatalities and serious injuries is to be applauded, and stands as a glowing beacon of inspiration for safety professionals world-wide, there is a danger that complacency can creep into business practice. Health and safety can be a hard sell for businesses and for global safety professionals – finding, fresh, innovative approaches to improving workplace safety is a tough challenge. This practical guide to safety culture urges readers to eschew traditional perspectives and instead take a practical, big picture view on safety. A refreshing and timely addition to the health and safety conversation.*
**Nick Warburton, Editor, Safety & Health Practitioner (SHP)**

*When most organizations find their safety performance stuck on a plateau, having exhausted technical and procedural controls, they usually move on to culture. But with so much hype about culture, how do you really move beyond the status quo and get closer to that goal of zero injuries?* From Accidents to Zero *delivers a thoughtful narrative that provides a wealth of practical ideas and actions to help expand your view, push the boundaries and allow you to successfully make that leap forward.*
**Subash C Ludhra CFIOSH, FRSA, JP, Former President of IOSH**

*From Accidents to Zero makes more sense than anything else I've read on safety culture. Sharman pushes us to think outside the box and this practical little book rocks my world.*
**Graham Redpath, Senior Project Manager, Emtelle**

# From Accidents to Zero

A Practical Guide to Improving Your
Workplace Safety Culture

Andrew Sharman

© Andrew Sharman 2014

www.andrewsharman.com

Published by Maverick Eagle Press.

www.maverickeaglepress.com

British Library Cataloguing in Publication Data.
A catalogue record for this book is available from the British Library.

ISBN: 978-0-9929906-0-2 (pbk)
ISBN: 978-0-9929906-1-9 (ebk)

Printed and bound in Great Britain.

Cover design by Juanita Gutierrez
www.juanitagm.com

Illustrations by Edwin Stoop, Business Visualizer at Sketching Maniacs
www.sketchingmaniacs.nl

**www.fromaccidentstozero.com**

*To Eagle#1, soar high!*

# Foreword

With this book Andrew has opened up the field of safety culture and broken it down into bite-sized components to facilitate new, critical thought and inspire practical action.

He brings a welcome challenge to the view that culture change is a long and difficult process by offering numerous pragmatic ideas to engage, motivate and drive positive evolution in the workplace.

As Chief Executive of the International Institute of Risk and Safety Management I am delighted to endorse this book. I am sure that you will find the style engaging and the content a useful nudge towards thinking differently about safety culture in your organization.

**Phillip Pearson**
Chief Executive
IIRSM

# Introduction

The world of work is changing, often setting the safety challenge in a new context – particularly in business. As leaders increasingly understand the importance of good safety practice to support their business objectives, safety and health practitioners continuously develop better tools and solutions. However it's clear that there is still a gulf between these groups. This is often explicitly expressed in terms of assurance, governance and reporting – but in reality it is about engagement, communication and understanding.

Andrew Sharman has engaged with wisdom from the world outside safety and provided us with 26 windows through which we can address this challenge in a new and imaginative ways. This book sets up the opportunity for all parts of any organisation to start these essential conversations and offers an invitation to take the first steps to acting differently. It sparks insights into how both traditional methods and novel approaches can be brought to life in real world situations.

Sometimes real progress requires the bringing together of developments in different areas of human endeavour. As such, Andrew's book provides us with a valuable service by making those links. I'm sure this book will be a valuable companion not only to the safety and health practitioner but also to their leaders and peers, for us all to move forward to deliver on our common mission.

**Jan Chmiel**
Chief Executive
Institution of Occupational Safety and Health

# Who is this book for?

You may have already made good progress with safety, reducing the number of injuries in your organization to an all-time low.

Or perhaps you find your organization's Accident Frequency Rates on a performance plateau.

You may be starting out as a safety professional, maybe you're a seasoned old hand, or perhaps you're someone with an interest in making things safer in the workplace.

Wherever you are, whoever you may be, at whatever point in your journey to zero accidents you find yourself, this book has something just for **you**.

# How to use this book

The first rule of how to use this book… is that there are *no rules* on how to use this book.

It's designed in a way that you can read any of these short chapters, at any time, in any order you wish. As a suggestion to get you started, have a look at the *Contents* page and see which of the chapter headings spark some excitement or interest in your mind, and begin there.

Or you could just flick the book open at a random page and start from that point. If you prefer a more traditional method, start at the beginning, and just keep turning the pages until you get to the end. Whichever way you choose, all I ask is that you approach these chapters with an open mind and a readiness for thought. A smile on your face from time to time will also work wonders.

As you may have already guessed from the title of this book, there are twenty-six chapters, starting with A, and ending with Z. Each chapter is short: the point being to articulate the key issue quickly and get you thinking. Nobel Prize Winner Daniel Kahneman recently published an excellent book entitled *Thinking, Fast and Slow*. Taking my cue from Kahneman, I'd suggest that you try *'Reading, Fast and Slow'*. Resist the urge to turn the pages quickly and 'complete' the book. Instead, pause a while, try to consider not just the words on the page, but also where they lead your thoughts. Take some time to let your mind wander, drifting from where the chapter started, through a web of connected thoughts and ideas of your own…

At the end of each chapter you'll find several questions. These are included to encourage you further into thinking critically about your current approach to workplace safety, to challenge your own beliefs, to push the edges of the envelope a little. The questions are an important part of each chapter so do try to spend some time reflecting on them. Feel free to jot down your thoughts in the white space around the questions, it's your book after all!

# Prologue

*From Accidents to Zero: A Practical Guide to Improving Your Workplace Safety Culture* isn't really a regular sort of safety book. It's not a reference guide to legislation, or an overview of management systems. It doesn't explain the complex mechanical workings or the deep scientific evidence behind a particular model of safety behaviour. And it won't attempt to pioneer a new one either.

This book is not a prescription for performance improvement: it does not cover *every* aspect of safety, or culture. Following the ideas shared in this book will not necessarily *guarantee* a reduction in workplace accidents – though many of the tools and concepts contained in the following pages *have* indeed had that effect in many organizations.

Yes, the title infers a reduction in accident statistics, but that's the intended *output* from this book – not our core focus. But if we direct our efforts to *align safety* with the business agenda, *engaging those around us* to bring forward their *contributions* and *collaborate*, this will <u>certainly</u> *result* in us moving closer on our journey from *Accidents to Zero*.

The aim of this book is to attempt to deconstruct some of the mystery that surrounds – and arguably has become – *'safety culture'*. It seeks to strip back the academic theory and the grey clouds of complexity to provide a critical and concise narrative that offers food for a thoughtful mindset in the hope that one or two of these short chapters will encourage an alternate perspective, a rational review, or even just a second thought.

This is not a safety course. I'm not expecting you to sit down and listen to what I have to say and nod your head sagely every few moments then go home. I don't expect you to agree with everything in this book. In fact I positively *want* to make you feel skeptical, provoke your thought and stimulate discussion.

The traditional view is that culture change takes a very long time. I don't subscribe to this theory. Culture change takes as long as we *want it to*. When we realize that culture changes <u>one person at a time</u>, we can understand that if we're prepared to put in the effort we can make a real difference very quickly indeed.

Toolbox talks, employee surveys, suggestion schemes, safety campaigns, posters, stand-downs, procedures, policies, quizzes, checklists, audits and protective equipment inspections have all had their day.

Sure there's still a place for them in the workplace, but they won't get you to where you want to go: **zero accidents**. Why not? Here's the secret: because most of the people in your workplace are <u>not thinking about safety</u>.

They're thinking about doing their work

They're thinking about doing a great job

They're thinking about their family and friends

They're thinking about their lives

Those traditional approaches are all well and good, but they fall short on one point – they make an assumption that all workers *want to* learn. We make matters worse by then insisting that workers *have to* do safety, that it's a *'condition of employment'*. It's The Rules. It's The Law.

*'Have to'* or *'want to'* – which is more attractive to you?

Right! So how do we *help* our colleagues to *want to* work safely? We need a different approach. And that's what you'll find in this book. Rather than pages of prescription you'll find discussions on behaviour, trust, mindfulness, values, and leadership. We'll talk about ways to involve, engage and motivate workers, to encourage collaboration and build a shared understanding of what corporate culture really is, why it's so important when it comes to workplace safety, and how we can harness its power to take us closer to our vision of a workplace that's *free from injury*.

There is no technical jargon in this book, and just minimal amounts of theory – certainly nothing heavy. What you will find, is over eighty new ideas, suggestions and actions for you to consider and try out in your workplace.

This book <u>isn't</u> about *preventing accidents* it's about <u>*creating safety*</u> in the workplace. You can make a difference, right here, right now, today. *Enjoy the journey!*

**Andrew Sharman**

# Contents

# Accidents

Accidents happen, right? Every minute of every day, someone, somewhere around the world is involved in an accident. Right now, as you read this line, a person you most probably do not know is about to be involved in an event that will likely cause them pain and suffering. Which for some of these people will continue for the rest of their lives. In one moment everything changes. It's not just the injured party either, the ripple effect touches family, friends, and many others. In the workplace everything stops. Machines are switched off, resources reallocated, investigations begin, root causes must be found. STOP. One just happened then.

It feels almost *too* simplistic to begin with a definition of a word that we use every day, doesn't it? But alas, it's exactly this point that provides a veritable bone of contention for all of our stakeholders – our leaders, our peers, our colleagues in different regions around the world – and without doubt no one more so that those who suffer accidents; the injured parties, and, of course, their families.

*So what exactly is an accident?*

Before we can prevent *accidents*, we must understand what we mean by this term. Is the occurrence of an intense storm that topples trees onto cars and houses an *accident*? Is it the event where a flock of birds is sucked into the engine of a jetplane causing it to stall? Is it the eruption of a volcano spewing ash into the air? Has one occurred when I reach for a tool at work and I feel a twinge in my back? Or the moment when a train misses a red signal and blasts through a level crossing just as the pedestrians finish walking across? I would say no, these may all be referred to as *incidents*.

What, then, should our definition be? Two common ones utilized around the globe are presented below, the first from the United States of America:

> *"An accident is an undesired event that results in personal injury or property damage."*[1]

And now from the workplace safety regulator in the United Kingdom:

> *"An accident is a separate, identifiable, unintended incident, which causes physical injury."* [2]

Yes, these are basic definitions but they give us a line in the sand from which we can work forward. At this stage in our discussion we could veer off into a deep debate about the difference between *accident* and *injury*, but this little book is constrained by size, so let's try to keep it brief. I'll use the two terms *accident* and *injury* interchangeably in this book because as we saw in the definitions provided above, an *accident* typically results in an injury. I do however recognize and accept that an *accident* may occur where there is no injury, but that some other form of damage – for example, to property – is sustained. The difference between an injury or no injury resulting from an accident may only be a matter of chance, so when we're thinking about our mission – moving *From Accidents to Zero* – let's take a holistic view and keep that broader definition in mind.

Why should we bother to investigate accidents? Beyond the obvious humanistic point, the answer is straightforward: we investigate in order to prevent accidents, and others like them, from recurring. Once an accident has happened it becomes a statistic, evidence, a black mark we can't wash away. But we *can* learn from it.

Accidents occur as a result of weaknesses in the control systems in place within an organization. These controls include procedures, physical measures (e.g. guarding, access control) and employee behaviour (at both operational and strategic levels). Logic tells us that if an undesired event occurs once, it is obviously possible for it to occur again. We investigate accidents to understand how and why they occurred. When we determine the how and why we can develop and introduce modifications to our control systems that reduce the chance of similar accidents occurring.

Later in this book we'll look at some of the classical models for accident investigation, but for now we can say that everything starts with obtaining a thorough understanding of the actions and conditions that led to the undesired event. A solid foundation for gaining this clarity of understanding begins with the *Five W* approach: answering the questions of *Who, What, When, Where,* and *Why*.

Once a basic understanding of the chain of events is achieved, we can begin to draw our initial conclusions. At this point in the investigation there are two vital rules to obey: the first, that we do not consider our findings to be absolute – there may still be issues that we have not yet identified. Second, we aim to keep the number of conclusions tight. So many times investigations that begin with a strong start break down at this stage by attempting to provide long lists of potential corrective actions. It's fair to say that the ability of most organizations to deal with such a large number becomes the challenge, and improvement in system predictability (remember that our ultimate aim is to stop similar events occurring) is considerably diluted. Key here is for us to *focus our attention on selecting the conclusions that are most relevant in preventing the adverse event to occur.*

With these primary conclusions identified, we can begin to implement corrective actions that can help us to significantly reduce the likelihood that the event will recur. As we undertake this task, it's precisely at this point that we have the potential to *maximize the value* to be gained from our accident investigation. Here's a simple example to illustrate this point:

> *Accident: A worker falls from a ladder that slipped out from under him. During the investigation the ladder is inspected and it is noticed that one of the rubber non-slip feet was missing from the ladder*
> *Conclusion: The ladder was not properly maintained*

Is the corrective action obvious to you? Sure, we fix the ladder by replacing the missing rubber foot, right? But wait, could we leverage this idea to prevent other accidents? Yes, we could implement a quick check of all ladders to be sure that the rubber feet are in place. But wait a moment, what else might this corrective action apply to? We could also check other access equipment such as stepladders too. Now we're talking!

An *even more* effective corrective action would be to establish a scheduled formal inspection and preventive maintenance process for all portable tools, including ladders. Now we are maximising the impact of what has been learned from the accident and *creating safety* in the workplace.

Corrective actions are the silver linings waiting to be uncovered by the process of accident investigation. Carefully identifying actions that will effectively reduce the risk of similar events recurring and implementing them appropriately will improve the reliability of your control systems for the future and move you forward on your own journey to zero accidents. Bear in mind that corrective actions should not only have impact, but should also be achievable – it's no use developing a list of corrective actions that the organization simply cannot complete. Finally, remember that unless you actually complete the corrective actions in a timely manner, your effort to investigate the accident will have gone to waste.

## Check it out

1   What is your organization's formal definition of an *accident*? Is this view shared by everyone in the workplace?

2   What could you do to ensure you maximize the value from each and every accident investigation?

3   Does your accident investigation process include a check or follow up to ensure that corrective actions are implemented and effective?

# References

1 https://www.osha.gov/SLTC/etools/safetyhealth/mod4_factsheets_accinvest.html
2 http://www.hse.gov.uk/riddor/key-definitions.htm

# Behaviour

As a whole, this book is about safety culture. It's specifically about providing practical ideas to stimulate thought and action to drive positive change in culture to the benefit of workplace safety. Typically, culture change has been thought of as a long, difficult, drawn-out affair filled with challenge, pitfalls and dead-ends… well, it can be if that's what you want it to be.

But it doesn't *need* to be like this.

You see, culture change is about *perspective*. Encouraging people to consider their attitudes and actions from a different angle.

Think for a moment about the last time you were in a bad mood… Perhaps something didn't go as you planned at work. Maybe you shared a cross word with your spouse or partner at home. Or the kids didn't tidy up after themselves. How did you *feel*? Now think about what you did next. How did you *behave*? Did you slam the door as you left the room? Thumped the table with your fist? Raised your voice? Vowed never to buy so many toys for the children? Or did you calmly smile to yourself and let it all go?

If we observe that our attitude affects our actions, then we can see that *behaviours* are what we do, how we act, how we react, how we inter-react. How we work. Who we are. Every minute of every day.

As our individual behaviours come together with those of others around us they collectively form and shape the *cultures* of the organizations (and family units, social groups and partnerships) we belong to. The oft-used definition of culture *'the way we do things around here'* may be considered too simplistic for many who prefer some complex pseudo-psychological alternative, but I think it's a great way to look at things – especially workplace safety. Because culture, as this definition explains, is all about <u>behaviour</u>. But as respectful human beings we know it's tricky to get down to specifics – especially when we are talking about individual people, so instead we amalgamate and talk in more general terms of groups, teams, departments, organizations. That's why we talk of cultures, but we then allow ourselves to be confused about how to influence and drive change within these cultures and return to our conclusion that culture change is hard work.

A lot of what has been written on the topic of safety behaviour – and culture – tends to focus on the deeper, academic and psychological aspects. The majority of this work is excellent, and as an Organizational Behaviourist, I spend many hours reading these works, exploring new concepts, models and abstractions. But, despite *how much* we know about the complexities of human behaviour, much of what ends up as 'Behaviour-Based Safety' ('BBS') products and tools just doesn't make a lot of logical sense to the average person. Therefore often it's distilled down to over-simplistic tools that are presented as effective and usable by anyone, anywhere. From a practical perspective, though, they don't quite cut it. As my good friend the Canadian safety guru Alan Quilley likes to say: *"safe behaviour is not a program. It's not a package of observation cards."*

In almost every safety book or journal we pick up, we'll be advised that up to 90% of all workplace injuries and fatal accidents are caused by behaviour. This figure always brings a wry smile to my face. Of course behaviours are part of the root cause of almost all accidents. Almost all accidents involve human beings!

Whilst good Safety Management Systems, policies, procedures and other tools have prevented hundreds and thousands of injuries at work, and brought accident and injury rates down for companies around the globe, many organizations find themselves on a performance plateau. Close, but not quite close enough to their target of zero injuries. It's usually at this point that these organizations shift their attention beyond engineering controls, such as machinery guarding, and administrative controls, like procedures and training courses, and turn to what they perceive to be the panacea – influencing behaviour.

Human behaviours are complex, dynamic, and subject to influence from a broad variety of factors. Rarely is a documented procedure sufficient to drive a sustainable change in behaviour. In the legendary paper by Judith Komaki and colleagues back in 1978, the results of perhaps the very first formal, concerted attempt to influence workers behaviours around safety were presented to the public. Since that time there have been many brilliant books written on human behavior. You can find many of these for yourselves, so I won't attempt to try to cover their content in this short chapter. Instead I'll try to encourage you to think about behaviour from a fairly straight-forward standpoint.

If our aim is to influence behaviours we must first understand and accept that it is very hard to force people to do things. Especially forcing them to do things they don't want to do. Think of how stubborn young children can be when asked to eat a particular vegetable – no matter how many times you tell them it's *'good for them'* the reluctance to put a piece of a certain veggie in their mouths just grows stronger.

So what do we do? A loop-the-loop aeroplane or *tssht-tssht-tssht* choo-choo train with the spoon or fork loaded with the good green stuff? Or we try to disguise the broccoli, peas, or carrots – hidden behind something tastier, or mashed up amongst the potato. One young mother I know has even resorted to adding food colouring in an attempt to coerce her little one into 'doing the right thing'. Perhaps we advise the child that they cannot leave the table until they clear their plate. Or ban the X-Box, Nintendo or after-dinner candy… Sometimes we may find these approaches effective, but not always. Why? Because the child simply does not <u>want</u> to eat the veggie!

The **Activator-Behaviour-consequence** (or 'ABC') **Model** of influence is highly popular within the safety sphere. It's a simple though highly relevant approach to explaining the important 'lead-in' and 'follow-up' elements of behaviour.

The model suggests that we always need an **Activator** (sometimes referred to as an 'antecedent') to drive behaviour in people. The activator is the thing that shapes our attitude towards something and *motivates* us to undertake a particular behaviour.

The **Behaviour** is the specific action taken by the individual *in response to* the activator.

And the **Consequence** is the result *emanating from the specific action* taken.

Look back at the ABC model again. Which of these elements do you feel we truly have control over and can actively manage? In the children's mealtime examples above, we can see parents trying to manage the activators (choo-choo trains) and the consequences (withholding dessert or playtime). The bit in the middle – the behaviour – remains under the choice of the individual involved. So in order to drive a particular behaviour we need to provide an effective activator to generate the required action, and then reinforce the action with a specific consequence.

My sister really gets the ABC model. Mealtimes in her house are typically preceded by playtime. Her two boys, Charlie and Max, are off having fun – making dens in the garden, playing pirates, or drawing pictures. As they arrive at the table for dinner, their mother asks them about their play activities and as they describe what they've been up to, their little minds are *activated* to recapture the excitement they were just absorbed by. Asking what the kids plan to do *after they finish* eating, she builds a potential *consequence* – or reward – perhaps of more playtime into the conversation.

At the end of the day, people, whether babes or adults, decide how to react. Just like feeding broccoli to our kids, we need to find ways to do safety *with* people, not try to force feed it to them. Our aim is to help people <u>want</u> safety. To influence behaviour, we can provide <u>relevant</u> activators and consequences that encourage individuals to think for themselves and react accordingly – ideally in the way we desire them to behave: *safely*.

Activators are everywhere in our daily lives – the sign on the highway warning you that you are entering a zone covered by speed cameras; the 'final call' message for your flight at the airport; even the 'wet paint' sign on the park bench. Each spark certain behaviours, all have consequences.

The three elements of the ABC are all equally important. Activators without Consequence may drive specific behaviours, but they may not be the ones we expect or want. Think for a moment, do you ever drive along a stretch of local road that features a sign warning you of speed cameras, yet you know from frequently driving this road that there are never any cameras on this route? How effective is this activator at influencing your speed? Now consider a behaviour without a specific activator. Let's use the same situation, but this time imagine there is no warning of the camera and days after travelling the route you receive a penalty fine through the mail, how do you feel? Yes, the frustration may lead to a specific behaviour to regulate your speed, but how effective is this approach?

We all benefit from reminders to act in certain ways. Whether it's the speed camera warning sign, or the message at the movies to turn off your mobile phone, activators can quickly and efficiently influence our behaviour in a positive way.

You won't have a safe workplace without safe behaviours. To get safe behaviours you'll need to address attitudes and beliefs. So to influence behaviours to create safety at work, instead of standing around staring at people trying to do their jobs and meticulously checking boxes on an observation card, how about trying to think how we might work *with* them to find helpful activators to <u>encourage the right behaviours</u>, and then provide a *desirable* consequence that reinforces that behaviour (or helps correct things when the behaviour is not as we wished for).

## Action stations!

1   Where have you noticed effective activators recently? As you drive to work today, wander round the shops, or enjoy some leisure time, try to observe how the ABC model is at play in the world around you.

2   Have a look at your workplace – do you have activators in place to drive certain behaviours? How effective are these? Where you feel activators are not working well, ask people why. Is your 'Wear Safety Glasses' sign ineffective because there are no glasses available, or because there is no consequence for those who do not wear them?

3   Consider the consequences you have in place. Are they desirable? How could you build positive incentives for safety into your workplace?

# Culture

What is culture and why does it matter to safety professionals? The answer to why it matters is simple; culture heavily influences an individual's behavior by setting group norms. Answering the first question is a little more difficult, but as this book is a practical guide, let's give it a go. In 1952, a list[1] of 164 definitions of *culture* was created, yet more than six decades later, opinions are still divided as to what the term means.

Ultimately, in a workplace setting, *culture* concerns the collective grouping of the organization to a particular way of thinking and acting in order to meets its prescribed objectives. This sense of strategic programming is often simplified to culture being:

> *"The way we do things around here."*

Although this is simple to get our heads around, it feels a bit vague. For this chapter we need something more solid to work from. Perhaps a more meaningful definition of culture is:

> *"The system of information that codes the manner in which the people in an organized group interact with their social and physical environment"* where the *"frame of reference is the sets of rules, regulations, mores and methods of interaction within the group."*[2]

Edgar Schein, former professor at the Massachusetts Institute of Technology spent his career studying culture in the workplace. Accordingly his definition may bring value to our discussion:

> *"Culture is a pattern of shared tacit assumptions that was learned by a group as it solved its problems of external adaptation and internal integration that has worked well enough to be considered valid and, therefore, to be taught to new members as the correct way to perceive, think, feel in relation to those problems."*[3]

Right, so now we've enjoyed the opportunity to exercise our grey matter a little, let's see if we can distil things down to the core essence. From a psycho-social perspective, Giddens offers that culture is the:

> *"…values that members of a group share, the norms they follow, and the material objects they create."*

Okay, it's becoming clearer. So culture is the way we do things, guided by the values that we hold dear and regulated by the methods and practices accepted in the workplace.

Now let's spice things up a little. We're here to talk about safety, so let's try to broaden our perspective. Definitions of *safety culture* are myriad. There may even be as many, if not more, than the number on that other list. Most contemporary definitions appear to be based on the one generated by the Advisory Committee on the Safety of Nuclear Installations following the Chernobyl disaster, so this is a good place to begin:

> *"The safety culture of an organization is the product of individual and group values, attitudes, competencies and patterns of behaviour that determine the commitment to, and the style and proficiency of, an organization's health and safety programmes."*

Whilst safety culture is acknowledged as an important concept, its content and consequences have enjoyed little consensus of opinion over the last few decades and an absence of models that specify relationships between culture, safety management and safety performance persists. Dialogue around safety culture has emerged as a popular theme in contemporary scholarship, usually as an answer to accident causation, and also as the silver bullet for performance improvement.

In modern times, the term is typically connected with the prevention of accidents, and it enjoys centre-stage as an approach to driving sustained performance improvement. But *safety culture* as a concept is not without conflict. Despite its popularity, and many attempts at its definition, the term remains an abstract concept and still remains vague. Indeed, even James Reason, one of the founding fathers of modern risk and safety management, suggests that *'few phrases occur more frequently in discussion about hazardous technologies than safety culture. Few things are so sought after and yet so little understood'*.

Fortunately, however, some definitions appear to be used more frequently by both researchers and practitioners than others, here's some of the most popular:

> *"The set of assumptions and associated practices which permit beliefs about danger and safety to be constructed"*[4]

> *"The embodiment of a set of principles which loosely define what an organisation is like in terms of health and safety"*[5]

*"The attitudes, beliefs and perceptions shared by natural groups as defining norms and values which determine how they act and react in relation to risks and risk control systems"* [6]

Although the term *safety culture* is now widely used and defined, it holds a relatively young pedigree. Following the Chernobyl nuclear power plant explosion on 26th April 1986 the International Atomic Energy Agency identified that the 'poor safety culture' at the plant was the primary cause of the accident. Subsequently, many other major accident investigations, including those looking at the Piper Alpha oil platform, the NASA Challenger space shuttle, and the Macondo Deepwater Horizon oil spill have pinpointed safety culture as a key contributory factor. It may be that the concept of *safety culture* has evolved as a direct response to such events.

Hang on, instead of tying ourselves in knots trying to define the term here, why don't you choose the definition you prefer and let's move forward and look at the different dimensions of safety culture.

We can view safety culture as a product of three interrelated aspects:

- **Psychological** aspects (individual and group attitudes, perceptions and values);

- **Behavioural** aspects (safety-related actions and behaviours);

- **Situational** aspects (policies, procedures, organizational structures and management systems).

Looking from this perspective we can see that *safety culture* is the result of how the formal and informal aspects of an organization's daily life influencing safety in either a positive or negative way. This influence is generated on two levels by:

- Setting the values and norms, and underlying beliefs and convictions, through which workers deal with or disregard risks; *and*

- Influencing the conventions for safe or unsafe behaviour, interaction and communication.

Safety culture is not only *similar* to organizational culture, but indeed an inextricable <u>part of it:</u> actively influencing attitudes, beliefs and behaviours of individuals with regard to workplace safety. Remove the word *safety* (and any iteration of it) from the phrases above and you can see that we're talking about the same thing we began this chapter with. Sure, we could easily spin off here into a heated debate about whether it's possible to have a discreet and separate *safety culture* within an organization but that would require tens more pages of space to do so. I'll leave it up to you to conclude for yourself, though offer one thought: if you could have a *safety culture* in your organization, wouldn't you also have to have – by default – a *quality culture,* a *production culture,* a *distribution and logistics culture,* a *marketing culture,* a *finance culture* and so on?

Not wishing to confuse things, it might just be worth a quick diversion from our discussion to briefly touch on an aspect we have come to refer to as *climate*. Organizational *climate*, especially related to workplace safety, has been the subject of much study over the last three decades, with several writers proposing its utility as a robust leading indicator for workplace safety. Interestingly, the term *safety climate* appears to be used as a synonym for safety culture, despite some argument that they are completely separate entities.

Academic researchers Sue Cox and Rhona Flin consider safety climate as a *'manifestation of safety culture in the behaviour and expressed attitudes of employees'* and this is consistent with Schein's view that *'climate precedes culture'* and is simply *'culture in the making'*. These statements resonate with my own personal view but I'll leave it to you to decide whether you agree, or whether you feel that we're really just talking about the same thing.

Okay, come on, let's get back on track. Often, the *desired state* of corporate culture (whether related to safety, or more generically) is presented in a series of vision, mission, policy and value statements, however these statements and the actual practice may not match. Why? Well, because in simple terms, we don't *create* a culture in an organization, it is already there. We can *develop* that culture, or refine it, or enhance it, or even attempt to change it, through the *adaptation* and *integration* that Schein speaks of, but we don't *create* a completely new one. Blindly overlaying aspiration across your existing culture is like laying a carpet over a wooden floor. The wood still exists: the boards still squeak as you walk over them and the woodworms and mites are still busy deep within the grain.

Really understanding your corporate culture and its nuances is vital. Purchasing an off-the-shelf audit, management system or behavioural safety program just won't cut it. Yet some organizations continue to forge ahead gleefully on this route, essentially *inflicting* a program or system upon themselves that just doesn't fit congruently with '*the way they do things*'.

Most of the main theoretical models of safety culture appear to have been adapted and enlarged from Schein's three-layered cultural model which reflects assumptions; beliefs and values; and behaviours, (though if you'll permit me to be critical for a moment, many such models frequently ignore the fluid dynamism of culture). Schein advocates that there are three components that serve to make up and influence culture: Organizational Artifacts, Espoused Values, and Underlying Assumptions:

- **Organizational Artifacts** are readily observable in the workplace and can include a particularly prevalent architectural or furniture style; dress code; artwork; symbols or graphics; communication styles and media; rituals, ceremonies or established events. Typically artifacts can be recognized by people internal and external to the culture or organization. Whilst tangible and easy to spot, the meaning of organizational artifacts is harder to decipher or interpret, though their impact can be significant.

- **Espoused Values** are not necessarily directly observable but can be distilled from how watching people behave. The espoused values are essentially how the workers at all levels choose to represent the organization both to themselves and to others. They may lie within the organization's stated beliefs, principles and mindsets or be expressed in official philosophies, public statements or rules. They may also form part of a vision of the future, of what individuals or the organization hopes to become, for example the popular maxims of 'safety first', 'zero accidents', and so on.

- **Shared Basic Assumptions** are the source of the organizational values and artifacts and form the essence of culture. They are the deeply embedded, taken-for-granted, behaviours which are typically carried out unconsciously. These assumptions are so well engrained in the organizational dynamic that they are difficult to identify and observe – even from within the corporation.

At this stage in your reading you may be starting to wonder how you can influence the culture in your organization positively towards safety. In order to build a framework to do this, I've studied the literature for you with the aim of identifying the main factors that influence an organization's safety culture. You can explore these further in this book, as well as during subsequent discussions in your own workplace. Whilst there appears to be no overall agreement on what the most important elements are, common themes and patterns do exist in the research.

Here's the top ten [7]:

- Management commitment

- Risk perception and management

- Safety systems and procedures

- Work pressures and scheduling

- Employee training and competence

- Genuine and consistent management of safety

- Clear communication

- Employee engagement and involvement

- Responsibility

- Regulatory compliance

So now we know that we need to consider the artifacts, values and assumptions of our organization and that there are ten key factors for us to work on if we are to build a solid, sustainable culture of safety, but how should we move forward?

You could start with a SWOT analysis to work out the Strengths, Weaknesses, Opportunities and Threats for action against those ten factors listed above. Narrow your focus onto the key areas that will really make the difference and you have a framework for action. Next, turn down the volume on the aspects of the old culture that you wish to change and turn up the bass on the new. Take every opportunity to reinforce the new assumptions, values and artifacts. Be an apostle. Recruit disciples. Keep your foot on the gas – remember the journey *never* ends.

## It ain't what you do, it's the way that you do it... [8]

1   Which definition of culture (or safety culture) resonates most with you? Do you think that the majority of your colleagues and co-workers would understand culture in the same way?

2   Look back at the list of the ten factors that influence safety culture. Which of these do you feel need most attention in your organization right now?

3   Take a walk around your workplace – what artifacts do you notice? What do these mean to you? Do you think that your view is congruent with the majority of people who work here?

4   Which values and assumptions within your organization are most relevant to safety at work? How could you use these to drive safety improvement?

# References

1   It's a fascinating read, have a look for the 1952 paper from Kroeber and Kluckhohn entitled *Culture: A Critical Review of Concepts and Definitions*.
2   Reber A.S. 1995.
3   Schein E.H. 2004.
4   Turner B.A. & Pidgeon N. 1997.
5   Glendon A.I. & Stanton N.A. 2000.
6   Hale A.R. 2000.
7   If you'd like to follow up on some of these themes in more detail, do have a look at the paper published in 2000 by Flin, Mearns *et al.*, or Mearns, Flin, *et al.*, 2001. Zohar's work in 2010 to review *Thirty Years of Safety Climate Research* offers a broad array of reflections and ideas for the future. Whilst finally, Kluckhohn and Kelly's excellent little book *The Concept of Culture* from 1945 is a worthwhile read to review how culture has evolved in itself.
8   …*and that's what gets results*. This tune was a big hit in the UK for Fun Boy Three in 1982. Even today it still gets me dancing.

# Daily Rituals

Every day begins the same for me. My alarm rings, I wake with a start, hop out of bed and aim for the coffee machine. That little green light signals it's going to be a good day and as the coffee starts to drip I dive under the shower. Mug in hand I wander to the window, throw it wide open and shout *"Bonjour le monde"* at the lake and the mountains.

In the office I start with the very best of intentions, beginning with a rough sense of what I want to do, I switch on my computer and am ready for the day. And then it happens. Before I know it, almost two hours have vanished on what I've now begun to call my 'daily admin'. That sea of red email that appears overnight is really a bowl of spaghetti: you start with one bit and somehow it's connected to loads more pieces.

In his time management courses Peter Bregman asks his students *"How many of you begin each day with too much time and not enough to do in it?"* Apparently no one has ever raised their hand. Could you? Nope, me neither. So as Peter says, we literally begin each day *knowing* that we simply won't get everything done.

In safety it's exactly the same isn't it? Have a look over there at your current strategy, your spreadsheet, Gantt chart, milestone planner or to-do list. Are you *precisely* where you want to be right now with your activities? We know that how we plan and spend our time are key strategic decisions, that's why we make these lists. Most of us are pretty good at list-building. It's the execution that's the real challenge.

So how do we achieve what we to set out to do each day, week, month, year? How do we ensure that we focus on those things that really take us closer to our goal of zero accidents and help us to build a culture that really values safety?

The answer is *daily rituals*.

My Great Aunt Sylvia had hers: a teaspoon of whisky in her cup of tea each morning was undoubtedly my favorite. She vowed that this was what kept her living so well for almost 100 years. Andy Warhol had his. So did Leo Tolstoy, Charles Darwin, Pablo Picasso, George Gershwin, Winston Churchill, Hannibal from the A-Team, and even The Fonz in Happy Days. Arnold Schwarzenegger still does. As we learned in the last chapter, Edgar Schein views rituals as essential. He considers them as *'organizational artifacts'* – vital components of corporate culture.

Almost every other book on management, self-development or wellbeing will tell you that the way most successful people excel in their work, live to be 100, or become insanely happy is through the process of habit. Working consistently and deliberately on specific things drives us ever-closer towards our goals.

We've all had experience of trying to build new habits. Usually we have a go around the first of January each year, and before the end of the month we realize things have gone off track. If we look into the reasons why such resolutions fail, top of the list is that we made them too complicated, or too onerous.

So let's give ourselves a chance here. Below you'll find some of the simple *Daily Rituals* that I use to help create safety in the workplace:

**Focus** – With my espresso in hand I ask myself *'What can you do today that will allow you to leave work this evening feeling like you've made a difference?'* I review my to-do list (for you it might be your strategy plan or wherever else it is that you keep your string of actions) and select the one – yes, just one! – item that I most want to achieve and then schedule this into my diary just like I would an appointment with a client.

**Safety Contact** – One of my clients, the DuPont corporation, is famous for this one. No matter who you are, or where you are in the business, every meeting begins with a moment for safety. Done right, it's an incredibly impactful way of focusing attention on your core values. These are not throwaway lines but something meaningful. I'll never forget the time I sat down to a meeting and a colleague opened the session by explaining that his two-year-old toddler had been struck by a car reversing on a driveway. The driveway was at my colleague's house. And he was the driver. From that moment forward I've parked my car facing forward to be sure I always have the maximum visibility before I pull away. I've also been at meetings where fear and embarrassment kicks in and the safety contact goes something like *"The company next door had an accident last night, so let's all be careful out there."* Good safety contacts are concise, relevant and action-oriented. They can come from within your own organization, or from beyond. If you're stuck, have a look at the newspapers – there's always something in there that can be used as a hook to get you started.

**Dialogue** – That song was wrong. It's not money that makes the world go round; it's conversation. Elsewhere in this book we discuss how, in order to build a strong culture of safety, we need to engage and interact with those around us, finding ways to encourage involvement and collaboration. Conversation is key. Every day, no matter where I am, I always stop what I'm doing and take five minutes to have a conversation about safety. Yesterday, Saturday, it was with some builders working on my neighbour's house. On Friday it was a tough-looking guy who had spent thirty years working in the steel mill. Like my morning coffee, if I don't get my daily dialogue I really feel like something's missing. There are millions of ways to structure this, but I like to keep it straightforward. Three questions, five minutes. After a polite *'hello and how are you'* it usually goes along the lines of:

1 *'What are you working on today?'*
2 *'If I were working with you, what would I need to know to be able to work safely?'*
3 *'How do you think we could make this job even safer?'*

I'm totally convinced that a positive safety culture grows <u>one person at a time</u>. It spreads like a virus, infecting others as we come into contact with them, and they pass it on to others. That's why I believe so much in the power of these short *daily dialogues.*

***Language*** – Following from the *dialogues,* here's another easy one: The research tells us that the more we talk about safety, the more it becomes apparent to those around us that it's important. But just chattering on randomly is neither effective nor efficient. Instead, if we can find a way to talk about safety constructively, in functional terms, we really underline what we mean. Alan Quilley shared a great observation when he asked me to think about the shop-floor conversations between managers and workers. A common question is often *"How quickly can you get that job done?"* By adding just one word to this sentence we can completely change the response we encourage in others. Have you guessed the word? Al's suggestion is that we change the question to *"How quickly can you get that job done <u>safely</u>?"* I've shared this idea with countless supervisors and managers, each of whom have been blown away by how simple is it to demonstrate their own personal commitment to safety <u>and still</u> maintain their focus on getting the products out the door.

***PAT*** – A former military friend of mine became known for his firm approach; he was a thoroughly no-nonsense sort of a chap. Despite whatever tough message he had to deliver to his comrades, though, Tim's little ritual was to always begin with the word *please* and end with *thank you*. For this he earned the nickname 'Pat'. In our busy lives 'PAT' is something we can easily forget, but its power is immense when used sincerely and consistently. Try it for yourself!

***Hourly Buzzer*** – Here's one I learned from Peter Bregman. I set the alarm function on my phone to beep on the hour, every hour. When the alarm goes off I stop what I'm doing, take a deep breath and mentally review those last 60 minutes. Have I really worked productively? Then I look at my *Daily Focus* and recommit to how I will spend the next hour. It's a very quick action that ensures that I maintain control over my day rather than letting the hours manage me. When you decide that you've achieved your *Daily Focus,* go back to your list and choose the next action to become your *focus.*

***Reboot*** – One of my personal favorite daily rituals is based on advice from my father. Dad tells me this is something he picked up as a young engineer. At the end of every work day, when you have decided that you have finished everything you wanted to do / could do today, clear your desk, put on your jacket, pick up your bag and start to walk out the door. Then stop. Return to your desk, sit down and reflect on the day. What worked well, what not so. Now write a list of the five things you want to work on tomorrow. Take no longer than five minutes to write the list and any accompanying notes-to-self. Then get up again and leave for the night.

When we do the same things each day, something mysterious starts to happen. A process clicks into place where, inevitably, the universe comes to our assistance. As Steven Pressfield says in *The War of Art* "*Unseen forces enlist on our cause; serendipity reinforces our purpose.*"

## Give us this day...

1   What rituals form part of your day? Which of these has a positive impact on safety?

2   It only takes thirty days for a new action to stick and become a habit. Which of the *daily rituals* described above will you commit to doing for the next thirty days?

# Evolution

I spoke recently at one of the global TED conferences[1]. The theme for the event was *perpetual (r)evolution*. As I researched and wrote my talk, I found myself exploring the difference between *revolution* and *evolution*. The more I read, thought, and wrote, the more I began to notice stark differences between the two concepts.

My conclusions led me to the point where I felt that *revolution* was like a wheel, rotating around a central axis. Spinning around and around, the wheel essentially retains the same shape, size, and function. On the other hand, the *evolution* implies a sense of forward progress, Whether we think of the evolution of mankind, mobile telephones, or approaches to safety, it's clear that standing still is not an option.

So how can we prevent our safety efforts from spinning around the same point? What are the secrets to building an approach that evolves as our organizational safety culture develops? I suggest that there are four key elements that we must focus our attention on: We must *encourage* people to get involved, *engage* them fully, *enable* them to work in safety, and *empower* them to take action. Let's look at each of these in turn.

### Encourage

Think about your own choices in life. Why do you do the things you do? I'll hazard a guess that there is almost always something that motivates you to take certain action. Now think about some of the new or unusual activities you've undertaken recently – perhaps you learned a new language, took up a new sport or hobby, stopped smoking, or visited a country or city you'd never dreamed of going to before. What caused you to do this? Perhaps there was some specific encouragement from someone or something that provided the initial motivation to act. In the workplace it goes the same way: without encouragement, people simply won't do some of the things necessary. Gentle encouragement is an effective way to focus attention on what's required and get folks ready to move in the right direction.

## Engage

My Canadian friend Alan Quilley specializes in driving a step change in safety across the shop-floor. One of my favorites lines from Al's repertoire is that *"You just can't deliver safety like a pizza in a box!"* Never a truer word said! We just cannot *do* safety *to* people, the only route to success is to *engage* people and work *with* them to identify challenges, solutions and approaches. It continues to amaze me just how many organizations invest huge amounts of time, money and resources developing very sophisticated safety improvement programs, campaigns and tools almost in secret within the H&S department only to be met with a lack of take-up by their workers.

## Enable

Once we have gained the attention of our audience, *encouraged* them to get involved and then gained their commitment to *engage* with us we need to equip them with the skills, knowledge and tools to *enable* them to work in safety. Enabling people isn't about *telling them* what to do, it's about building the competence and confidence to allow them to understand how do it for themselves.

## Empower

We learn something from everything we do, and we use these experiential learnings as we face the next challenge or action that crosses our path. Where we find things that go well, or bring us positive results, we tend to repeat the successful actions. Generating the space to allow people to practice what we've asked of them is crucial.

Change is the new normal. Whether we like it or not, as human beings we are constantly evolving, day after day after day. As Charles Darwin pointed out way back in the mid 19th century:

> *"It is not the strongest of the species that survives, nor the most intelligent... It is the one that is the most adaptable to change."*[2]

Research confirms that there is a far stronger correlation between worker involvement in safety and incidence rates, than there is between compliance and incidence rates. Compliance and control is not sufficient on our journey to reach zero accidents. We need to move beyond compliance being the goal and instead find ways to encourage interaction and facilitate empowerment.

Creating a great safety culture requires *evolution* not a *revolution*.

## Rolling forward

1   Are you 'delivering pizza' or do you fully engage the workforce? How is safety approached in your organization?

2 How do you ensure that your people are adaptable to change when it comes to matters of workplace safety?

3 Do you provide the necessary space to enable people to develop the required safety skills and knowledge? How can you empower them to take action?

# References

1 If you're not already familiar with the TED concept, visit www.ted.com. To view my talk – on fear, risk, safety and swimming with sharks visit http://youtu.be/B7-DQFvD5ck or click the TED link on my website at www.andrewsharman.com.
2 Charles Darwin's book *On the Origin of Species* is considered to be the foundation of evolutionary biology. First published in 1859 its choice of language may present a little challenge from time to time, but it is without doubt fascinating.

# Felt Leadership

The traditional view of culture change is that it is deemed to be effective only when <u>everyone</u> is involved, from the boardroom to the shop-floor. Every leader, every manager, every supervisor, every frontline worker.

Of course this sounds like a wonderful situation… but frankly it's nonsense.

I would not argue against the notion that 100% engagement of the entire workforce would be beneficial in many respects, but I don't believe that it has to be an *'all or nothing'* approach to influencing safety behaviours.

In his magnificent and highly provocative book *Viral Change*, psychiatrist Leandro Herrero explains that culture change works <u>one person at a time</u>. Herrero tells us that change is <u>most effective</u> when it spreads like a virus. Step by step, gradually infecting everyone. Just like catching the common cold from that guy sneezing next to you on the subway this morning. When we realize that effective change comes from this individualized action, not only does developing a positive safety culture feel more achievable, it actually becomes more practical to manage too.

*'Felt leadership'* operates in exactly this sort of viral change process. It's not necessarily a new style or theory of leadership; instead we might consider it the distillation of the some of the more impactful elements from a range of schools of thought on leadership. It's essentially about *'walking the talk'*, demonstrating that management commitment to safety is as strong as it's claimed to be. In my view, it's the foundation for building trust and supportive relationships at all levels within the organization. Done well, felt leadership moves an organization from a focus on compliance to a deeper, more cultural approach, based on shared commitment.

Over time, many organizations have found that their safety cultures have been considerably enhanced through the application of felt leadership, benefiting not just workplace safety performance, but also delivering sustainable, shared value to other areas of the business too.

Strong, visible, management commitment is the basic component of any successful safety management system and this commitment must start at the top, permeating down through all levels of the organization. To achieve zero accidents, leaders must sincerely believe that safety is as equally important as any other business aspect – such as quality, productivity and cost.

Leaders must bear in mind that their attitudes, behaviors, actions, inactions and examples will all be viewed as illustrations of their personal level of commitment with respect to safety in the workplace. What we say, speak and write must be visibly reflected in what we do.

So how can we prove we're committed to safety?

Felt leaders:

- Set a great example

- Understand the business operations

- Anticipate risks

- Discuss hazards with employees and within peer groups

- Are alert to unsafe conditions in the workplace

- Inspect the workplace frequently and intelligently

- Take effective corrective actions

- Investigate incidents and accidents

- Maintain discipline

- Know their employees, their needs and aspirations

- Make safety part of the everyday business

As we said in the previous section, for leadership in safety to be 'felt' by those around us, leaders must hold an absolute personal commitment to the organization's value on safety.

In our own research, three safety values in particular were found to recur again and again. It's worthwhile to take a look at these now:

- All workplace injuries and ill-health are preventable

- Everyone has the right to go home safely at the end of every day

• Safety is a line responsibility that is owned, led and driven by the entire team of leaders within the organization

These values act as the blueprint for felt leadership. Acknowledging that safety is a core business value, and integral to the very existence of the organization, is crucial for setting the scene, and when demonstrated through the actions of leaders can have a profound effect on employees.

How can we utilize the concept of felt leadership in our organizations? After more than 200 years of focusing on safety the DuPont organization understands that felt leadership is a critical part of any safety management system.

DuPont uses ten straightforward principles to guide them on their journey to safety excellence:

1   Be visible to the organization

2   Be relentless about your time with people

3   Recognize your role as teacher/trainer

4   Develop your own safety skills and pass them along to the organization

5   Behave and lead as you desire others to do

6   Maintain a focus on the safety of oneself as well as for others

7   Confirm and reconfirm safety as a core organizational value

8   Place continuous emphasis and clarity around safety expectations

9   Show a passion for zero injuries, illnesses, and incidents

10  Celebrate and recognize success

These principles are for everyone: felt leadership in safety is not the exclusive domain of senior executives. Whilst commitment must start from the top, all levels in the organizational hierarchy can spread the safety change – just like the cold virus. The ten principles shared above are as relevant and useful to the new team member as they are to the CEO.

In summary, we can see that felt leadership is an action-focused, transformational approach that builds strong safety cultures through the inter-relationships between leaders and followers. When felt leadership is demonstrated within an organization in the area of safety, a cultural transformation can occur. More importantly, that transformation becomes sustainable as it becomes part of the fabric of the company and the work environment.

Remember that safety excellence is a journey, not a destination. Along the route you'll get the level of safety performance that you as a leader personally demonstrate that you want.

As a rule of thumb, remember that felt leadership:

- Is easily observable

- Demonstrates a personal commitment

- Makes a positive impression on employees

- Involves all levels of employees

- Affects all levels of employees

## Can you feel it?

1   Test yourself against the ten principles of felt leadership – where do you feel that there is room for improvement?

2   What objectives do you have built into supervisors, managers and leaders work plans that measure the impact of their felt leadership?

# Groups

Whether we like not or not, whether we admit to it or not, we all act differently when we are in the company of other people compared to when we're on our own. Other people, especially in the form of *groups* of other people, have a tremendously powerful impact on human behaviour. Why should this be so? Aren't we always the same person?

Cast your mind back to last weekend. You woke a little later than you did through the week, ignored the alarm clock on its first call, and then padded through to the kitchen for your wake-up hit of espresso. It was a double-shot because you'd enjoyed a couple of drinks the night before to celebrate the end of a tough week. Catching a glimpse of yourself in the mirror you notice your hair sticking up, and your 'lucky' pajamas – a bit threadbare, but super-comfy. You slump into the sofa and idly flick the remote. Aaah, nice! Saturday morning and you're all alone. It doesn't matter what you look like or what you're doing. After a while you become aware of someone else moving around but not so much as to break your concentration from the morning's sports results / cooking programme / cartoons.

Suddenly you notice your partner staring at you. You spring to attention, run your hands through your hair in a bid to smarten up, switch off the television, and sprint off for a shower and set of clean clothes.

Not the case for you? Okay, then I'll either congratulate you on your long and joyous marriage where your partner accepts everything that you are and do without comment, or I'll help you to celebrate your independent life without responsibility! So, if the previous example didn't apply to you, let's try another – just for fun. Imagine you're at a party, reaching for a well-deserved cold beer, when a stranger asks what you do for a living. You turn to see several people standing around, waiting for you to reply. How do you respond? Change the question to *'what type of music do you like?'* if you prefer. Or switch the situation to a date with someone new – think about the effort you put into selecting 'just-the-right-outfit'. Case closed: we <u>all</u> indulge ourselves with a little 'impression management' every now and again.

Social psychologists have known for years that when we're alone we feel much more relaxed and less concerned about our general state. But as soon as one other person is added to the mix, we quickly become much more aware of our environment and our appearance. Doing things like combing our hair, choosing an outfit, or other simple tasks can be done with a relative ease – and often a higher level of performance – when others are around (ever noticed how quickly you can get ready when your partner is waiting in the other room to take you out on a nice date?). But in tasks with a greater degree of complexity, or new activities that we are not accustomed to, we strive harder in order to impress those around us, and ultimately, our level of performance actually reduces.

Let me give you an example. Near to my house there's a pathway that runs along the lakeside. It's perfectly smooth, level bitumen, and I often see people cruising along it on their rollerblades. In the spirit of 'becoming cool', I decided to give it a go – after all, how hard could it be? The first time I went out on my 'blades was a Monday evening. Around 8.30pm and the path was quiet, no-one was around. I skated a little, fell over a lot, but without witnesses I felt okay and carried on. A couple of hours later and I was feeling pretty relaxed with my new hobby. A few days later I decided to skate into town for a coffee. At 5pm on a sunny afternoon the path was filled with parents and pushchairs, joggers, kids on bikes, and people on rollerblades. My first few steps were unsightly: a two-metre tall giant with arms and legs flailing wildly as he struggled to stay upright. After my first couple of heavy crashes to the ground my confidence was dented. *Everyone* was watching me. Or at least so I thought. Then I began to notice it wasn't just my rollerblading technique, but also my quirky costume – running leggings with shorts over the top, the clash of colours, the jaunty bandana… On my third crash to the ground I quickly tugged off my 'blades and tiptoed home, out of sight. No matter what we are doing, when we think we are being observed, our confidence quickly gets the better of us. In new tasks (like my rollerblading) this can cause us to give up, but in well-learned actions (like the next night when I took my kayak out for a paddle) our confidence in front of others grows and this can help improve our performance. This concept – known as *social facilitation* – has several forms. Let's explore a couple of them now.

### Groupthink

As a safety professional have you ever attended a meeting where you left the room wondering what had happened? Had an effective decision had just been made or was it simply a case of general consensus being achieved?

On the 20th of April 2010 the Deepwater Horizon rig exploded in the Gulf of Mexico claiming eleven lives, numerous injuries and hundreds of negative environmental impacts. Prior to the explosion, senior leaders had visited the site to celebrate several years without a significant safety issue. So what went wrong? In his meticulous review of the tragic event, Professor Andrew Hopkins [1] reveals that *groupthink* was rife within the engineering team responsible for the platform. In the early 1970s, research psychologist Irving Janis identified that in groups of people that tend to agree on most issues that cross their paths, their level of collective confidence increases to such a level that a sense of blissful harmony is formed. The group members appear to like each other, and instinctively agree with each other – often without needing deep explanation. As levels of agreement rise within the group, when an opposing argument is brought to the table, *groupthink* is the pressure applied to quash dissent and bring the detractor into line with the majority in a misguided bid to preserve unity, loyalty and team cohesiveness. Ironically, it's precisely this cohesiveness (or interpersonal attractiveness and liking, in simple terms) that has been shown to have a positive impact on team performance and also team member satisfaction, however strong levels reach a tipping point which pushes the group towards dysfunction. *Groupthink* can manifest as subtle actions like persuasion or apparent rationalization by the majority, to more direct forms such as public ridicule or torment. No matter the format, *groupthink* essentially acts as a psychological bulldozer to clear the way of anyone with an opposing view who dares stand up and block consensus.

Is *groupthink* a common issue? Well, the research tells us it can occur in any team where there are one or more of the following factors:

- Strong leadership

- Unstructured decision-making processes

- Pressure to find solutions

- High levels of group member homogeneity

- Limited input from external parties

- Self-managing teams

From a safety perspective, the effects of *groupthink* can be catastrophic. In January 1986 *groupthink* was found to one of the main contributing factors that led to the space shuttle *Challenger* breaking apart just 73 seconds into its flight.

The power of a group is defined and shaped by the collective beliefs held by its members. This shared view on the collective efficacy of the group has been found to be a significant predictor of performance and success. In *groupthink* situations leaders may appear to rely on the support of safety experts. On one hand this may seem like a strong position to be in as the technical expert advisor however the reality is that this causes us to be positioned upon a knife-edge. Walk the line and enjoy absolute followership but slip to one side and the impact of getting it wrong could be catastrophic in terms of personal credibility and for operational risk management.

**Group Polarization**
The likelihood of taking poor decision-making with regard to risk increases within a team or group environment. Whether in the Boardroom or at a Bachelor Party,

the power of influence by majority opinion can cause what social scientist Daniel Isenberg calls *'risky shift'* or *'group polarization'*.

Isenberg suggests that there is a downside to teams, in that a process of social comparison occurs as group members feel compelled to accept the more attractive views held by influential members of the group. For example, at the outset of a decision-making process or discussion some members of the group may have only slight opposition towards a particular issue, but the opinion of key individuals in the group can quickly cause amplification that can result in the group shifting their view in entirety. This situation is most likely to occur in teams that have established strong belief in their own ability – like in the boardroom of a successful organization, or perhaps on an alcohol and adrenalin-fuelled Bachelor Party.

*Group polarization* around matters of safety can manifest as a tangible response of *'risk immunity'* – that feeling of corporate invincibility – with phrases like *'it never happened to us before so we'll probably be fine in the future'*. Or it may appear as 'discounting', where current risks are acknowledged by leaders but underestimated in terms of their likelihood and severity. Taking these positions ignores the uncertainty that lies between action and effect. Precaution can evolve into a false virtue as *'better safe than sorry'* becomes the maxim of choice, whilst at the opposite end of the spectrum *groupthink* takes over and undermines...

## Optimizing group activities

In their meta-analysis of 17 studies on culture across a range of industry sectors and countries Rhona Flin and her colleagues concluded that objective management was the primary theme connected to developing a robust safety culture[2]. But in a challenging industrial era we are naturally anxious about change and uncertainty, and it's easy to find consolation in the solidarity that a group can bring. Group goal setting is a tool that can really help to avoid the risks of *groupthink* and *polarization*. Where goals are set by the team acting in concert – as opposed to goals prescribed by an individual – a shared sense of ownership is created which catalyzes greater effort, encourages persistence, and increases the likelihood of achieving the goals. If the goals for your team (or the team you'd like to influence) are already set, don't despair; you can strengthen the team and increase your chances of avoiding the pitfalls of group dynamics through the application of several other useful actions and principles:

- Agree rules on decision-making

- Open and participative leadership

- Brainstorm in smaller teams then review output in the broader group

- Rotate team members

- Appoint a 'Devil's Advocate' position to challenge and present alternate points of view

- Regular inclusion of a range of external inputs from outside the team

- Ask each member to list a pro and con for their viewpoint

- Remove the final decision maker from the group, allowing them to withdraw to consider their objective decision

## Help the group to think

1  Do you see evidence of *groupthink* or *group polarization* in your organization? Where does this happen and why?

2  How could you introduce an opportunity to create and agree some group goals around safety in your organization?

3  Who are the most influential members of the groups that you frequently interact with? How can you help them to form objective opinions about safety in the workplace?

## References

1    Hopkins, A. 2012.
2    Flin R, Mearns K, O'Connor P & Bryden R. 2000.

# Hawthorne Effect

*"I think, therefore I am.*
*You watch me, therefore I am better.*
*You watch us, we think, therefore we all improve."*

When 16th century French philosopher Descartes first uttered the words *"je pense, donc je suis"* *("I think, therefore I am")* could he have known how much impact his proposition would have in the centuries to follow? Translated from the original French to gain wider audience, Descartes' *cogito ergo sum* quickly became a staple of Latin studies around the world. His proposition is regarded by many as one of the core foundations of modern philosophy. It certainly serves to remind us that we are all thinking human beings. Scholars offer that *cogito* is necessary before we can move forward in our lives and lies at the heart of performance improvement. With apologies to Descartes, *cogito* can be taken a step further – as my addition to his quotation above suggests.

Employees of the Western Electric Company were certainly thinking human beings when Australian sociologist Elton Mayo turned up at their factories in Hawthorne, a suburb of Chicago, USA in the 1920s.

Mayo and his crew wanted to study the effect of physical work conditions on productivity. In fine scientific rigor two groups of employees were the subjects of the study – one group was exposed to variations in lighting within their production areas, whilst the second (the 'control group') worked in an area where the lighting remained unchanged for the period of the study. The expectation was that those working with enhanced lighting would be more productive.

Day after day the lighting was gradually increased and the research team observed dutifully. As anticipated, the productivity of workers in the highly illuminated group was found to improve. Brilliant news: now, just by improving workplace lighting businesses around the world could maximize productivity. It must have been an exciting conclusion!

But when reviewing the data for the group being observed in the regular work area, the researchers found that their productivity had also improved – without the additional lighting. When the study ended Western Electric management reported that the productivity of the group with the enhanced lighting fell back to previous levels. Rethinking their hypotheses, the scientists advanced that productivity increased not due to the changes in the work environment, but because of the attention levied on the workers by the research team.

The 'Hawthorne Effect' as it has become known, refers to the tendency of some people to work harder and perform better when they are aware that they are being observed. Individuals appear to change their behaviors as a direct result of the attention they receive.

Is it really this simple? Mayo himself felt there must be more to it. The research team returned to Western Electric in the 1930s and became fascinated by the informal employee groups that seemed to appear within the formal structure of the company. By exploring the beliefs and creeds which make individuals feel part of an integrated group Mayo concluded that beyond the power of observation was the importance of group dynamics:

> *"The desire to stand well with one's fellows, the so-called human instinct of association, easily outweighs the merely individual interest and the logic of reasoning upon which so many spurious principles of management are based."*

Mayo's studies at Western Electric revealed that it was this sense of team spirit, based on unwritten codes of conduct within the group formed by and within themselves that determined the output of individual workers. Whilst the work environment may be important for comfort and wellbeing, the desire for groups to be seen to be efficient and effective was a greater driver for action.

The Hawthorne studies provide two key learnings for those interested in improving safety at work:

- The act of observation in itself has the power to influence human behaviour. As thinking human beings, we, as individuals usually appear to want to be observed, quite literally, in 'the best light'.

- Beyond 'looking good' as an individual, people take pride in demonstrating their efficacy and contribution in a group.

## Lighten Up!

1  Think about the process of observing workers in your organization. Are your workers acting so as to be seen in 'the best light'? What happens when the light stops shining on them? Does their behaviour change like the workers at Hawthorne?

2  How could you encourage the formation of strong bonds, positive beliefs, creeds and unwritten codes of conduct within your work teams?

3  What opportunities do individuals have to feel proud to be part of the team?

# Inattentional Blindness

Have you ever visited one of those all-you-can-eat buffet restaurants where there seems to be an endless array of delicious-looking food just waiting for you? If you're anything like me you may begin by having a look at what's on offer and then fill your plate with the items you love or that look especially appealing. When you join your friend back at the table, you notice that they seem to have one of your favorite dishes on their plate. You ask where they got it, only to be told that it was being poured into the buffet bar right in front of you. You missed it.

The classic example demonstrating *inattentional blindness* is that video clip with the gorilla. Did you see it? Psychologists Daniel Simons and Chris Chabris recreated a study originally designed in 1975 by Ulric Neisser where a scenario is set up comprising two basketball teams passing the ball around. A person wearing a gorilla suit wanders onto the court, thumps his chest and wanders off. In trials conducted by the team at Harvard University typically around 60% of viewers do not see the gorilla. How could this be possible? Before the clip is played, the viewers are asked to count how many times the ball is passed within a certain team. They expect to see the ball moving between players and focus on this task so intently that the gorilla is simply not noticed.

*Inattentional blindness* is not a cognitive or visual defect. It's essentially an issue of awareness – principally the failure to notice an entirely visible, though unexpected object because our brains are otherwise engaged. There's a limit to what our brains can cope with you see. In deciding where to focus, our brain scans around 30-40 pieces of data (sights, sounds, smells etc.) every second until something grabs its attention. It then filters out what it feels is important and the rest gets left behind.

The gorilla video excited so many people that Simons and Chabris produced a sequel in 2010. In this second movie viewers were ready and expecting the gorilla to appear. Sure enough it did, but viewers were so intent on looking for it that they missed several other unexpected events, such as the curtain in the background changing color.

How can it be that we continue to miss so many significant events? When choosing where to focus its energy, the brain applies four filters:

- **Capacity** – Our capacity to pay attention is essentially down to our mental aptitude and influenced by a range of factors including age, education, distraction, fatigue and drug or alcohol consumption.

- **Expectation** – Past experiences shape our future expectations. As an example, when I asked why employees in a food factory did not respond to the warning alarms on a production line they told me that because the alarms go off with such regularity but are usually 'false alarms', they now didn't notice them at all.

- **Mental Workload** – The perceptual loading of the brain increases the likelihood of *inattentional blindness*. Chances of error increase when our attention is diverted to a secondary task, for example filling in an online form whilst holding a conversation about an important subject.

- **Conspicuity** refers to the degree to which an object or information jumps out to command our attention. Our brains are drawn to sensory conspicuity – the contrast of an object against its background – like a bright red car on a sunny day on the highway, or cognitive conspicuity where we are more likely to notice something particularly relevant to us – for example the same car as the one we are driving on the highway.

When applied, these filters can bring great benefit to us, such as blocking out distractions to allow us to really concentrate. But because most of us tend to be unaware of the limits of our attention, we take on other activities whilst engaged in primary tasks, and it's here that the real risk lies when it comes to safety. An example is using a mobile telephone whilst driving. For many people, making a call whilst driving is *perceived* to be an acceptable task, convinced that they would notice a sudden event occurring, but even with the bright red flash of brake lights…

Next time your accident investigation draws you to conclude that the individual involved was negligent, careless or 'not paying attention', just take a step back. Studies have shown that even the most attentive, intelligent and vigilant people would suffer the same degree of *inattentional blindness* in similar situations. So consider the four brain filters carefully and see whether you notice any gorillas.

## Look, See!

1    Analyze the most common types of accidents in your workplace to see if you can find any evidence of *inattentional blindness* occurring.

2   Review the four brain filters listed above against your accident analyses – how could you reduce the risks through interventions around conspicuity, mental workload and expectation?

# Just Culture

Along our journey to safety excellence things might not always go as smoothly as we plan. Accidents may occur, right? We know that each one provides us with a unique opportunity to learn so that we can take appropriate action to prevent their recurrence. If we miss this chance, we really lose out. But so many organizations minimize the value they could gain from these incidents due to the way their culture responds to them.

Key to developing a robust culture of safety is clarity: knowing what's going on at every level of the organization. Transparency rocks. We know that it's important that all accidents, incidents and near misses are reported, and that sufficient processes are in place for the investigation, development and implementation of suitable preventative actions. But if we truly want our employees to provide us with this information we need to *create* an environment where they feel able to step forward and offer their thoughts and opinions freely and for these to be received openly and respectfully by the organization. Any process we use to do this must be easy to use, respect confidentiality, and be worthwhile.

An organizational climate where news of negative safety events such as accidents, injuries and near misses is met with disappointment and unease is not conducive to a developing this clarity – in fact it drives things in the opposite direction – into the dark depths, underground. Reporting is quickly minimized, provided only when forced or extracted, and near miss events tend to be dismissed as accidents *'avoided through the skill of experienced workers'*, or simply, sheer luck.

As part of sharing learnings from their accident investigation process a leading global player in the manufacturing industry would distribute a newsflash to all sites summarizing every significant incident that occurred. Not a bad idea you may think. Not so good if you were the one suffering injury though, as your name and photograph would feature in the first few lines of the report. As you might have already guessed, it wasn't long before the company found themselves with zero accident reports – though a corresponding spike in unexplained absence suggested that the statistics may not have been totally true.

Organizations which place emphasis on identifying fault and apportioning blame will <u>always</u> encourage a culture of fear and embarrassment which will sooner or later lead to under-reporting when it comes to safety issues. At the opposite end of the spectrum, an organization attempting to operate a totally blame-free work environment is likely to suffer willful neglect and violation frequently. Finding the balance is our aim, and *appropriate accountability* is the route to success.

Balancing our desire to learn from mistakes with the need to take corrective action to reinforce the notion of accountability is the way forward. In safety terms, thanks principally to the work of Sidney Dekker[1], this has become known as a *just culture* and can be defined as a culture in which individuals are not punished for actions, omissions or decisions taken by them that are <u>commensurate with their experience and training</u>, but at the same time, where gross negligence, willful violations and destructive acts are not tolerated. Whilst it discourages *blame*, it's right to note that a *just culture* is <u>not</u> a *'no-fault'* system. It doesn't mean we have to operate under the auspices of *'no blame'* – attribution of fault has an important function – but rather we incorporate a sense of fair and appropriate accountability into what we do. In a *just culture* there is an acceptance and understanding that human errors are often caused through system failures (as opposed to, but of course in addition to the potential for, personal failures) so it's vital that all accidents, issues, concerns and failings are investigated equally and proportionately.

In simple terms, a *just culture* is about being objective, rational and fair rather than jumping to conclusions on the first nuggets of information we receive. If we are thorough in our accident investigation processes and really strive to identify what went wrong, we will most likely often find that the majority of unsafe acts and behaviours that have occurred boil down to being *unintentional errors* rather than deliberate wrong-doing. Thorough and systematic evaluation of events is key and investigations into where things have gone awry should include determining whether the actions were as intended, whether an individual knowingly violated procedures or policies, and whether there is a history of such violation.

In his latest brilliant book Dr. Tim Marsh, one of the pioneers of behaviour-based safety in the UK, draws the distinction between human errors and violations:

> *"In order for there to be a violation, there must, by definition, be a rule and secondly, a deliberate intention to break it. If there's no rule, then no violation is possible!"* [2]

In fact, even when we look at those that are considered to be *violations*, we may often find that such willful incorrect actions have been quite literally catalyzed in the individual's mind due to organizational pressure (real, implied or perceived) or an internal self-influence of wanting to *'do the right thing'* – like meeting the day's production target before the end of the shift. Where the mistake was inadvertent or occurred in a system that was not supportive of safety (such as a period of extended, mandatory overtime leading to fatigue, for example), an appropriate response in a *just culture* would include coaching and education. Of course, malicious or purposefully harmful behavior must not be tolerated and individuals should held responsible for their actions within the context of the circumstances in which they occurred.

Operating a *just culture* allows people to concentrate on doing their best work – rather than worrying about watching their backs, trying to limit their personal liability. It embraces the notion that people are fallible and <u>will</u> make mistakes from time to time. This type of work environment positively encourages a sense of shared ownership where individuals feel free to support workplace safety improvements by identifying weaknesses and failures in the system, and stepping forward when errors occur. A *just* approach is that sweet spot which helps us to:

- Galvanize commitment and engagement

- Promote safe behaviours

- Reduce the frequency of unsafe acts

- Increase transparency

- Build trust

- Increase objectivity in analysis and decision-making

- Contribute to learning and continuous improvement

- Balance accountability with safety

- Increase openness of reporting

- Enhance motivation

Being *'just'* is a crucial element in developing an organizational culture that values safety, engenders employee engagement and builds robust meaningful leadership. As Dekker reminds *"Being able to offer an account for our actions is the basis for a decent, open, functioning society."*

Without a *'just'* culture we just won't know what's going on.

## *Just* do it!

1   Do you feel that you *'know what's going on'* in your organization with regard to safety incidents? What gives you confidence that every event is being reported?

2   How do you build objectivity into your accident investigation process? What measures do you have in place to encourage people to step back and make a thorough and impartial evaluation of the events that occurred?

3   It can be easy to perceive a legitimate error as a willful violation. How does your organizational culture draw the distinction between them?

4   Examine your recent historical accidents: can you categorize them between errors and violations? Which is the majority? What does that tell you about your culture?

## References

1   Dekker S, 2007.
2   Marsh, 2014.

# Kahneman

Okay, so we're starting with a slightly abstract title for this chapter. But by the time we reach the end, I do hope that you'll understand why Kahneman[1] is the King of the K's on our little journey to *Zero Accidents*.

In 1974, Daniel Kahneman and his partner Amos Tversky made a ground-breaking discovery. Through their research they identified that the human brain was capable of taking mental short-cuts to solve problems or issues that we are faced with. A 'heuristic' to give them their proper name, is by Kahneman's own definition:

> *"A simple procedure that helps find adequate, though often imperfect, answers to difficult questions."*[2]

Heuristics are the little 'rules of thumb' that allow us to quickly process and conclude an efficient decision without having to pore over information or deliberate what our course of action should be. It's interesting to note that the word heuristic is derived from the same root as the word *eureka*. Perhaps this reflects exactly why, when our minds make these little short-cuts for us, we feel so pleased with ourselves for being so quick-thinking.

Kahneman and Tversky suggested that there are three main types of heuristics, and as their theory remains solid to this day let's take a look at each of them now.

***Availability Heuristics*** help us to estimate the probability and likelihood of something happening based on information we can recall. Studies suggest that those events we can bring to mind quickly and easily are those which have occurred most recently. For example, if the news reports several road accidents on a certain stretch of highway, then we may believe that we are more likely to suffer a crash on that particular road and avoid that route for the near future. Or if we sustain a number of forklift truck incidents in the workplace, we may believe that generally there is a high probability of another forklift incident occurring and focus all of our attention there.

**Anchoring Heuristics** are based on the idea that we often take decisions related to specific reference points within our memory. These reference points act as anchors to connect historical information to the present. As an example, if a manager in your organization was involved with a serious fire situation earlier in her career, future discussion on this topic will often trigger her thought process to pull against this anchor in her mind. This may result in either a raised level of awareness and knowledge, or conversely, perhaps a degree of over-sensitivity and a reluctance to engage.

Heuristics can be useful, but we should be minded to note that they can also lead to errors. Have you ever 'gone with your gut' only to find you made the wrong choice? This is because heuristics are imprecise ways of judging probability. As Kahneman says, they are a *"consequence of the mental shotgun, the imprecise control we have over targeting our responses"* to the questions or issues we face.

**Representativeness Heuristics** help us to predict the probability of something happening based on the proportion of relevant items in play. For example, if I take a jar of coloured candies, some red, some blue and ask you to tell me which colour of candy will be drawn next from the jar, you would no doubt want to know how many of each colour I had placed in the container. When I tell you that 75% of the candies were red, you would likely guess that red would be the colour of the next one to be drawn. This proportion is known as the *base rate*.

The *representativeness heuristic* is significant in our world of safety. Where a *base rate* appears to be in our favour we can be lulled into a false sense of security – for example, when we experience a period of time without an accident at work. Our confidence begins to grow and it becomes easy to believe that we have the ability to predict random events (accidents, or blue and red candies) from the *base rate* data to hand (our chart of historical rates or the data I gave you on sweets in the jar).

I noticed a busker on a street play with the *representativeness heuristic* recently. With a crowd gathered around him, he tossed a coin into the air. Six times in a row the coin landed 'heads-up'. He paused and asked a member of the audience to bet a dollar on the next toss. The audience clamoured to participate, and one man handed over his dollar, adamant that the coin would have to land showing 'tails' because it had landed showing 'heads' too many times already. The coin was tossed and landed. 'Heads' again! The crowd went wild and a sharp-looking lady moved forward from the edge of the group. Handing over a five dollar bill she exclaimed that she would bet 'heads'. The showman took the bet and flipped the coin. 'Tails' this time. Despite both participants having inspected the coin before each toss, and presumably noting that it indeed did have two sides and therefore a 50/50 chance of landing on either, they both appeared resolute that the odds were in their favour. *Representativeness heuristics* had taken away their capacity to think – and their dollars.

**The Affect Heuristic.** In his excellent book, *Thinking, Fast and Slow* Kahneman graciously introduces a new heuristic, proposed by psychologist Paul Slovic, where individuals allow their personal preferences and biases to influence their decisions. When the *Affect Heuristic* kicks in, our brains respond to our most basic emotional likes and dislikes. For example, if you observe a man with tattoos on his arms you may label him a thug, rebel, or perhaps a motorcyclist and might conclude that he is *'not your cup of tea'*. But the *affect heuristic* does not shut down your mind completely; it leaves the door open just a crack for you to change your decision. So when you learn that the man is in fact an eminent doctor who is known for saving the lives of many sick children it becomes easy for you to modify your initial view. Slovic and his peers have conducted several studies looking at *affect,* all of which confirm the bias most humans have for the physical appearance of others. In one recent study several participants were sent individually to make a sales pitch to a group of strangers. In each case where the participants were considered to be 'highly attractive' and 'well-groomed', the pitch was successful and the deal closed. Those participants who appeared to have taken less care with their choice of clothes and personal grooming rarely got the sale.

By their very nature, heuristics are used without our conscious thinking. The idea of a mental shotgun makes it easy for us to come up with fast answers to difficult situations because it avoids the need for long, deep thought. But like the coin used by the busker, heuristics have a flipside. They may lie behind the unconscious errors that we create as we go about our daily business and lead us into taking decisions and setting targets rather naievely.

## Mental gymnastics

1   If we use last year's accident rates as a heuristic to predict our performance this year, or five years into the future, is it a solid short-cut? What other data do we need to bring into consideration?

2   When we respond to an incident based on its pull against an anchor embedded deep within our memory, is our reaction proportionate?

3   If we calculate probability based on a spate of recent events how confident are we that we've got the numbers right?

4   When we provide commitment and support only for safety projects proposed by attractive members of the team, are we focusing on the right risks?

## References

1   Daniel Kahneman won the Nobel Prize in 2002 for his work on human judgment of risk and decision-making under uncertainty. He is regarded as one of the world's leading minds in psychology.

2   Kahneman, D. 2011.

# Leadership

Before you begin to read this chapter, let me ask you to stop for a moment.

Take a break, empty your mind.

Now, close your eyes and take 60 seconds to try to imagine what it would look like if your organization was in *'safety heaven'*.

How was that? What did you imagine? What did you see?

· *Were people carrying out their tasks safely?*

· *Employees working together on safety issues?*

· *Did you see managers asking for feedback and ideas?*

· *Senior directors taking an active and genuine interest in their teams?*

· *Did you hear the Chief Executive speaking about safety with real passion?*

· *Were employees leaving at the end of the day with a sense of pride?*

· *Did everyone look healthy, happy and free from injury?*

For most people it takes a bit of effort to imagine this idea of a 'safety heaven'. However, achieving it doesn't need to be difficult. <u>Leadership</u> is how we get there.

The first step is what you just did. Being able to envision, define and describe where we want to go is key to <u>creating</u> the culture we dream of. This is what's come to be called *Transformational Leadership*. Vision, dynamism, energy and charisma are all hallmarks of this leadership style. Attentive to the needs of their stakeholders (or 'followers') *Transformational leaders* paint clear pictures to inspire action and they celebrate success with enthusiasm.

Next we need to <u>embed</u> the culture. We do this using a variety of techniques such as praise and recognition, coaching and corrective action. *Transactional leaders* are expert at identifying and driving action. They use their skills in communication, facilitation, planning and supervision in order to *'get things under control'*.

Then it's all about <u>sustaining</u> the culture. Keeping things going in the right direction. It's at this point that the smart leaders realize that a different style is required. *Servant Leadership* is the art of facilitation. At its most fundamental it's asking *'How can I help you?'* and then delivering the support that's necessary to enable people to work effectively towards their goals. Characteristics of a servant leadership style include commitment; listening; empathy; awareness; persuasion; conceptualization and creating a sense of community.

Research confirms that transactional and transformational leadership styles can be effective at engaging people and encouraging safe behaviours, but it is only servant leadership that has the power to create and sustain the supportive work environments necessary to develop both employee engagement <u>and</u> positive behaviours concurrently.

When we learn that leadership is a set of skills and abilities that can be developed in every individual, we typically try to select one style of leadership that we feel is most relevant to ourselves, our role and our aspirations. After reading the previous paragraph you may already be thinking *'how do I develop myself into a Servant Leader?'* However on our journey to develop a strong culture we must be mindful that just *one style of leadership* is insufficient. We need to be able to span all three styles – *transformational, transactional* and *servant* – if we are to truly build safety successes within our organization.

Let's break it down. At it's most fundamental, *leadership* is about relationships built on *trust, credibility* and *competence*. Given that safety is a *social activity* that involves everyone, it's imperative that we think carefully about these relationships.

- If we don't build relationships based on trust with the people we seek to lead, it's unlikely that they will follow.

- If our stakeholders don't view us as credible, they are unlikely to follow.

- If we are not regarded as having the competence to lead in the right direction it's unlikely that they will follow.

Benjamin Franklin understood the importance of consistent leadership and believed that the setting of a good example was key to building credible, trust-based relationships. The former President of Pennsylvania, USA remarked that it *'takes one thousand good deeds to build a reputation, yet only one bad deed to lose it'*.

Our journey towards a positive, sustainable culture of safety is, like Franklin's own journey, one where transactions and transformations are driven by collaborative relationships and result in win-win situations for all involved. So how do we develop the attributes necessary to lead effectively?

This book aims to be a practical guide to help you approach your vision for improving the safety culture in your organization. So let's do some real-time action-planning right now. Grab a piece of paper. Fold it in half, and then fold it again so that you have quartered the page. Open it back out and you have four boxes. Now draw a line from left to right, across the top of the page – running through the very top of the uppermost two boxes. On the left, above this line write the title '*Leaders*'. Over on the top right, above the line, write '*Attributes*'.

In that top left quarter box you have, under the column marked '*Leaders*' add the title '*The Best*' and list the best leaders that have been in your life. We're not talking about the managers you've worked for, but those people who you have considered to be *leaders* in the truest sense. They might be managers, bosses, executives in companies you've worked at, or teachers, professors, relatives, or maybe colleagues in your team. You may have even been inspired by a leader indirectly: perhaps a politician, academic, or other figure in the public eye. Add them to your list.

Once you have your list, begin to think about what it was about these leaders that impressed you so much. What were the particular character traits and actions you admired most about them? Write these down in that box over there on the top right of your sheet of paper.

Halfway done. Now in the bottom left box, yes, you guessed it, write '*The Worst*' and repeat the process. List the names of the worst leaders you've encountered. In the box to the right list the characteristics of these people that make you feel this way. As an example, here's one from my own experience:

| LEADERS | ATTRIBUTES |
| --- | --- |
| **The Best**<br>Bill Johnston<br>Jack Jones<br>My father<br>Graham<br>Mrs Scorgie<br>Rev. Ryrie | - Inspired me to give my best<br>- Provided space for me to learn<br>- Always polite and courteous<br>- Able to articulate where we were going and why<br>- Listened carefully to me<br>- Challenged constructively<br>- Acknowledged contributions of others<br>- Asked for my opinions and ideas<br>- Strong technical expertise |
| **The Worst**<br>Derek Hardman<br>Professor D<br>Sarah Smith<br>GT | - Screamed and shouted constantly<br>- Dictatorial style<br>- Never available for help<br>- Believed his answer was always the best<br>- 'JFDI'<br>- Didn't listen to others' ideas<br>- Played the 'I'm the boss' card too often<br>- No respect for others |

So what's the point of this little exercise? Well, like the sheet of paper you just used, it's twofold.

First, as individuals we quickly form biases towards the sorts of people we like to be led by, and those we don't. There's considerable research that shows that the characteristics of leaders in each of the two groups is remarkably similar for most people – meaning that most of us tend to like the particular leadership styles (or traits), and dislike certain others. No surprises – most folks are appreciative of leaders who listen, respect, care what we think, and involve us. We tend not to like those who only believe in themselves, appear selfish, and communicate rudely.

Secondly, even though we *know* (or at least could guess) what works for most people in terms of leadership styles and attributes, the way we often try to lead with safety may appear to those around us more like the things listed in the bottom right box.

Let's draw this chapter to an end with some ancient Taoist wisdom. As Chinese philosopher Lao-Tzu wrote in the 5th century BC:

> *"The highest type of ruler is one of whose existence the people are barely aware. Next comes one whom they love and praise. Next comes one whom they fear. Next comes one whom they despise and defy."*

## Lead on!

1   Think about your own natural preference for a particular style of leadership – do you tend to lean towards a transactional, transformational or servant style? Is this always the best option or do you see opportunities where switching between the three styles may be more effective?

2   Go back to your sheet of paper and review the two boxes on the right side. How are you leading safety? Like the best leaders you know? Or are there some aspects of the worst in there? It's never too late to change! What do you need to do?

# Mindfulness

.

During his teachings Buddhist Thich Nhat Hanh often remembers his deep experience of washing dishes; explaining how, at the beginning of his training, at Tu Hieu Pagoda in the 1940s, this task was far from pleasant. Washing the dishes for over one hundred monks each day, without soap but using ashes from the fire, and scrubbing using only rice and coconut husks. Cleaning so many plates and bowls must have indeed been a laborious chore! He recalls how the cold water drawn from the well was a slow task that chilled his hands to the bone – especially in the dead of winter. Even heating up a large pan of water sufficient for cleaning took some time. Once he had everything prepared, the challenge of scrubbing, wiping, cleaning, drying and stowing away such a volume of dishes in time to rejoin the other monks for practice meant that the task was always completed hurriedly and without a second thought.

Thirty years after these initial experiences in the '40s, Hanh contemplates the 'evolution' of washing dishes; amazed at the invention of hot running water from a kitchen tap, liquid soap and the array of special pads and brushes designed for scrubbing plates, bowls, pots and pans in the most efficient way. These *'advancements'* meant that even with a sizeable pile of bowls waiting to be washed, it would only be a matter of a few moments of time before he could sit down and relax with a cup of jasmine tea. Hanh's completion of the task was still not necessarily regarded as pleasant. And again it was completed with haste.

Now in the 21st century many of us may find ourselves fortunate enough to have a machine especially designed to wash and dry our dishes for us. Now all that remains is the simple task of stowing our plates and bowls within the machine, adding some detergent and pressing a button to commence the program. Still, the task is performed with speed, and without specific thought for what we are doing.

Even in a task as mundane as doing the dishes, Hanh advocates that we deprive ourselves of a magnificent opportunity:

*"While washing the dishes one should only be washing the dishes, which means that while washing the dishes one should be completely aware that one is washing the dishes."*

Acknowledging the simplicity of this thought Hanh accepts that it may seem strange to place so much effort on such mundane chores, however offers this this is exactly the point. By taking the time to deliberately focus on such a facile task (such as washing the dishes) one can become part of the moment, be oneself, conscious of our presence, thoughts and deeds. By simply taking part in the task mindfully, we are prevented from being *"tossed around mindlessly like a bottle slapped here and there on the waves."* In articulating this lesson to a colleague years later, Hanh explains that there are *"…two ways to wash the dishes."* The first is to *"wash the dishes to have clean dishes"* and the second is to *"wash the dishes to wash the dishes."* If we wash our dishes only to be able get to that cup of tea, or to rush to the next task that awaits us, or to simply *'get the dishes done'*, then we are not *"washing the dishes to wash the dishes."* Beyond this, Hanh even argues that we are *"not alive"* during this time. Our state of mental ambiguity standing at the sink will continue on to our tea drinking, as our bodies move automatically on to the next task on our list, and so on. In this way, our life spins out ahead of us as we become sucked away into the future. Our response is a constant attempt to play catch up.

Thich Nhat Hanh encourages us all, whether washing dishes or whatever we are doing, to be *mindful*. His excellent little book *The Miracle of Mindfulness* [1] skillfully blends Buddhist wisdom with modern pragmatism, and offers several simple exercises for increasing mindfulness in our daily lives. It's well worth a read.

In 2012 there were 477 scientific journal articles published on the topic of mindfulness. Right now in 2014, a *Google* search of the term returns over 6,340,000 results. Despite frequent mention in popular newspapers, magazines and an array of new book titles, mindfulness is not in itself a novel idea. Around the beginning of the third century AD the Anapanasati Sutra of Mindfulness states that:

*"When walking, the practitioner must be conscious that he is walking. When sitting, the practitioner must be conscious that he is sitting. When lying down, the practitioner must be conscious that he is lying down. No matter what positions one's body is in, the practitioner must be conscious of that position. Practicing thus, the practitioner lives in direct and constant mindfulness of the body…"*

I'm a big believer in the concept and the power of being mindful and urge you to take a moment of *mindfulness* – just for yourself – right now. During this chapter your mind may already have been considering having a go at mindfully washing the dishes. If this is your choice, go right ahead. However, if you have no soiled dishes waiting to be washed, or you might prefer something a little more… *enjoyable*, please try the following exercise. It should take you no longer than three to five minutes.

*Take a bar of chocolate; any flavour or variety you usually like is fine. Place it on the desk or table in front of you and spend thirty seconds observing it. Look carefully at the packaging, noticing the colours, branding styles, words and fonts used. Look at the size and shape of the bar. Resist all temptations to rip it open!*

*When you are sure that you have taken in all that can be observed, lift the bar into your hands, feeling the wrapper and the chocolate inside. Does the packaging feel smooth, sliding easily between your fingers? How is it finished – is it heat-sealed or folded simply? What do the colours evoke in your mind? Fully appreciate the bar.*

*Now, open the wrapper slowly and carefully, trying to cause as little damage to it as you possibly can, and avoiding damaging the contents. Break off a small piece of chocolate and hold it between two fingertips. Bring it close to your eyes and look carefully at it, examining its details, the finished edge, and where it has been broken away from the rest of the bar.*

*Draw the chocolate closer to your nose now and inhale its aroma. Do this several times whilst your mind considers the shape, size, colour and texture of the chocolate in your fingers. When you are ready, place the chocolate on your tongue and, resisting the temptation to immediately chew and swallow, allow it to melt slowly. Focus all of your mind on the taste, trying to discern the subtle flavor notes in your mouth and as it flows into your throat.*

*When the last taste of chocolate has left your mouth, reflect on the experience. How do you feel? What did you notice from this exercise?*

Now think about how you *usually* eat chocolate. Do you typically grab a bar as you leave the store, supermarket, coffee shop or gas station, and then quickly eat it as you race to your next appointment, or whilst trying to type an urgent response to an email you have received? Or perhaps jam the chocolate into your mouth as a fast food alternative to lunch because you just don't have the time to stop and eat?

Whether eating a chocolate bar, breakfast, lunch or dinner, we may all find ourselves guilty of rushing through the process, unaware of the full depth and breadth of the experience available to us. A bit like Thich Nat Hanh rushing through his chores of washing dishes. Could it be that when we engage in safety activities we do the same? Think back to the last safety observation you made, or perhaps the last safety meeting you attended (or chaired), or the behavioural observation feedback you offered to a colleague…

In *The Miracle of Mindfulness*, the Buddha recounts the story of *mindfulness* of the self, and its benefit to those around us:

*"There was once a couple of acrobats. The teacher was a poor widower and the student was a small girl. The two performed in the streets to earn enough to eat. They used a tall bamboo pole that the teacher balanced on top of his head while the little girl slowly climbed to the top. There she remained while the teacher continued to walk along the ground. Both had to devote all heir attention to maintain perfect balance and prevent any accident from occurring.*

*One day the teacher instructed the pupil: 'I will watch you and you watch me, so that we can help each other maintain concentration and prevent an accident. Then we'll be sure to earn enough to eat.' But the little girl was wise and answered, 'Dear master, I think it would be better for each of us to watch ourself. To look after oneself means to look after both of us. That way I am sure that we will avoid any accidents and will earn enough to eat.'"*

Thich Nhat Hanh endorses this lesson by suggesting that if in a family environment there is one person who practices *mindfulness*, then the whole family will both benefit from this *and* become more *mindful*. The presence of the member who lives mindfully serves as an active reminder to the others in the family to live in *mindfulness*. In a similar way in the workplace, when one person works with safety *mindfulness*, this can serve as a powerful reminder to his or her colleagues too.

## A moment of reflection

1   As we learn more about the art of *mindfulness* it quickly becomes apparent that the benefits of being mindful are myriad. Teachers like Thich Nhat Hanh and many others often advocate being *mindful* <u>every minute of every hour of every day</u>. In reality however, this may take some time for us to achieve.

2   So perhaps to begin, we might consider taking one day of the week to increase our *mindfulness*. Why not begin with a day of *Safety Mindfulness*? Begin with a short breathing exercise, inhaling and exhaling slowly to a count of three: *'Inhale, one, two, three'* and *'Exhale, one, two, three'*. Repeat this five times. Then, when you are ready, mindfully prepare yourself to move into the workplace by selecting and wearing the appropriate safety workwear or protective equipment. Now observe the work environment in the same way you did with the chocolate bar, carefully examining each area and aspect. Take the time to consider what you see in the context of safety, and then, only with the benefit of careful thought, decide your actions – whether to observe a co-worker, to begin a dialogue with a colleague, or to engage in a work activity in *total mindful safety*. Aim to continue your *mindfulness* throughout the whole day, using all of your senses to be alive in each moment and, as Thich Nat Hanh might have said: *'work in safety to <u>work</u> in safety.'*

# References

1   Hanh, Thich Nhat. 1991. The Miracle of Mindfulness. London: Random House.

# Near Misses

In 1931, Herbert Heinrich published his theory now commonly known as 'Heinrich's Law' or 'Heinrich's Triangle' which states that for every 'serious' workplace injury there are 29 'minor injury' events and 300 'no injury' events, or, as we might call them today, '**Near Misses**'. Heinrich proposed that by identifying and taking action on the 'no injury' events, actual injuries could be avoided.

38 years later, Frank Bird offered his own ratio, suggesting that for every serious injury, there would be 10 minor injuries, 30 events involving property damage, and a further 600 'no injury' events, or Near Misses.

These 'Accident Triangles' may present persuasive data, perhaps, but what actually is a Near Miss? The UK health and safety regulator, the Health & Safety Executive, suggests that a Near Miss is *"any incident, accident or emergency which did not result in injury."* Meanwhile the American Occupational Safety & Health Administration (OSHA) suggests that *"Near Misses describe incidents where no property was damaged and no personal injury sustained, but where, given a slight shift in time or position, damage and/or injury easily could have occurred".* More concisely, Collins American English Dictionary defines a Near Miss as *"a narrowly averted collision or near escape".* Gaining consensus on what a Near Miss is may be as challenging as defining 'good weather', however Near Misses have certainly found favour in recent times with safety culture models and Behaviour-Based Safety programmes – founded on the premise that up to 95% of all accidents are caused by unsafe acts or conditions – often incorporating a campaign or initiative to identify the Near Misses in a given workplace.

On one hand, this seems like a productive exercise – after all, what could go wrong with encouraging people to seek out those things that could cause injury or damage?

Taking things a step further, the UK Health & Safety Executive now indicate that there may be as many as two million unsafe acts or near misses per fatal injury. The explosion on the Piper Alpha North Sea oil platform in 1988 killed 167 people –

were there really 334 million Near Misses prior to this tragic event? When the Costa Concordia cruise ship ran aground in January 2012, 32 passengers lost their lives. Could 64 million Near Misses have been reported on board in the months prior?

Accident triangle ratios will of course vary between organizations; those starting out on a safety culture initiative may find themselves 'collecting' many more Near Misses than an organization which is much further along the maturity path. Ratios may vary due to the behaviours of the workforce and, may also hinge upon the leadership, influence, trust and relationships between line manager and employees. They may also vary based on the type of work environment – for example, would you expect more, or less Near Misses at a nuclear power station, or in a call centre? Why?

But are the actual numbers or the ratio truly that important? I suggest not, but in fact it's the 'overall picture' that tells the story. As we will see in other chapters of this book, looking in *isolation* at one measure or **indicator** is rarely helpful, and, at the end of the day, there will *always be some kind of ratio between your numbers*. Instead, the general shape and form of your 'accident triangle' may be more useful. Simply expressed, beginning at the foundation of the triangle with Near Misses, we should expect to see a steepening of the sides of the triangle as it moves through each tier, and, ideally, to its apex with **zero** fatal injuries.

However, caution must be applied – clear and robust definition, not just for Near Misses, but for the classifications of each tier of the triangle are crucial. Sharp attention is necessary to encourage objective review of the data, rather than striving to 'match' the ratios suggested by Heinrich or Bird. Bear in mind, though, even with apparently 'useful' data homogenized to 'triangle' form, there is no definite way of knowing which of the unsafe acts or near misses will result in a serious injury.

Whether based on Heinrich's or Bird's data, the 'Accident Triangle' model can be a useful tool for many OSH practitioners, and indeed many organizations, as it provides an easily understandable, adaptable, and quickly updatable, visual tool that can be used in most, if not all, workplaces. Certainly the triangle model has caused controversy and prompted debate over the years – for example, over whether Heinrich's data from 1920's accident reports remains valid in these modern times – however rigorous academic research has statistically substantiated the relationship between tiers of the triangle models and, most importantly, underlines a positive connection between employee involvement and safety performance.

So, isn't encouraging workers to get involved and identify and report Near Misses – however you choose to define them – a worthwhile and prudent step in the right direction?

Before you go and make a start, let's just check one more thing please. Over the last two decades I've been involved in setting up Near Miss reporting programs in many organizations. In each of them I've observed degrees of very real reluctance from employees to get involved. Here's what I've found to be some of the biggest barriers to reporting Near Misses:

- **Fear** – Some workplaces seem to have created a culture where workers feel punished or ridiculed when they suffer injury. A manager I worked with used to call one worker a 'frequent flyer' because he had so many accidents at work. In this sort of environment, workers typically resist reporting Near Misses for fear of being branded in similar ways.

- **Complexity** – One of the world's largest manufacturing companies spent millions on developing an online Near Miss reporting system, installing brand new computer terminals and smart signage on the shop-floors of every factory. Six months later, with only a handful of Near Misses reported they knew something was wrong. Eventually they learned that the new process was just too complicated and time consuming for workers to use. Keep it simple!

- **Peer Pressure** – No matter the industry, workers are a tight-knit bunch. Being the one who always reports Near Misses may cause ructions within the team. No-one wants to be regarded as the 'tell-tale' and in macho work environments this can be a real barrier. Reputation rules!

- **Apathy** – When workers know that the company doesn't empty the Near Miss box every day they understand that the business doesn't take Near Misses seriously. When Near Misses reports are not acted upon for several days, weeks or if at all, the message is amplified.

- **Bureaucracy** – Each month in a leading FMCG organization, the *Most Significant Near Miss* was selected for sharing across the business. The reporter would be asked to develop a deck of six slides explaining the issue and suggestions for resolution. The deck was then emailed to every manager to share with their teams. To encourage reporting, the worker filing the Near Miss of the month was awarded with a suitably branded baseball cap. Three years later and the company still has almost the entire stock of those hats… [1]

## Sharpen your focus

1   Create an Accident Triangle for your organization using current data to establish the ratio between serious injuries and Near Misses. How does your data compare to Heinrich and Bird? Did your data create a true 'triangle' shape? If not, why not? What could be the cause of another shape (for example where there are less Near Misses than 'minor' or 'serious' injuries)?

2   Review your organization's definition of 'Near Miss' against the actual Near Misses being reported. Do they match?

3    It's all too easy to concentrate on the events where people suffer harm and forget the 'non-injury events'. Try turning your Accident Triangle upside down and inverting your data – could this be a useful way to drive a sharper focus?

## References

1    I'm not totally against incentivizing safety, and feel strongly that we should reward proactive suggestions to improve safety should be rewarded rather than for number of hours, days, weeks or months worked without injury.  Of course, the choice of incentive is crucial too, as that FMCG company found out!

# Observation

In other chapters of this book we've talked about the power of observation. When we reflected on the work of Elton Mayo and his research team at the Hawthorne factory of Western Electric, we saw that the act of observation was enough in its own right to cause a short-term improvement in performance. However as this book is designed to be a practical guide to improving your safety culture, I'm not about to suggest that you should have people standing around watching others all day every day!

Culture is all about behaviour, and before we start trying to influence behaviour, we really should begin with understanding what the current behavioural patterns are like. This is where observation comes in. There are many proprietary tools available on the market now to help you build a format for observations, several of which come complete with little pre-printed notecards with prompts for what should be observed. These may be useful to you in your own journey to improve safety, but they're not essential. You can build your own template – or, for those feeling brave, why not ditch the idea of a proforma and instead think about the behaviour and the communication best practices you would want your observer to display.

What's the point of observations? Observation visits can help us to gather information that supports us to improve the way we work and make things safer. This information can also helps us to avoid events that could cause harm to our people, our business and our environment. They're also a great way to demonstrate that safety is important to the organization and its leaders. Current research indicates that around 85% of what we learn comes from observation of our peers, and as little as 5% from the formal training we receive. The power of positive observation is enormous!

In this chapter we'll walk through a process that will help you think about safety observations in your organization. Before we begin though, it's important to note that the act of observation is just one step in a broader activity. Yes, sure you can just march up to someone at work and stand and watch them, but I suggest that this may not be the most effective approach. In fact, more that that, it may be downright damaging to your safety culture! Being mindful about how you observe, and the process you use, will certainly bring better results, and ensure that all parties – observer and the observed – feel at ease.

## 5 Steps to Great Safety Observations

### 1. Be brave
One of easiest way to make an impact during a safety observation is to pussyfoot around. I recently noticed a manager gingerly hanging around on the edge of a work area, acting remarkably similar to a cat burglar considering how best to make off with the loot he's just snatched. After a full minute checking that the coast was clear, he locked his sights on a poor unsuspecting employee and hesitantly approached. During his approach he appeared to abort his mission twice. Third time lucky and the connection was made with the worker, who by this time was thoroughly confused about this leader's intention. Plenty of impact. All negative. Nothing arouses suspicion and fosters a lack of trust more in the workplace that a manager who looks like he doesn't know what he's doing. Yes, it's easier for managers to sit tight in their office, behind the urgent spreadsheets and workplans, but getting out of the comfort zone and onto the shopfloor is critical to success. It's likely that you will have to talk with people you may not know well. You may hear information that is difficult to take because it may generate more work for you. Be brave.

### 2. Plan
Safety observations are not about wandering round smiling and shaking hands. They are not PR exercises. They require careful thought, preparation and skill. Before you step foot on the shop floor ask yourself:

- Where will I walk?

- What will I likely encounter?

- Who will be there?

- What are their roles?

- What safety events have happened here recently?

- What story can I tell to break the ice?

- What am I aiming to achieve?

Prepare yourself for the observation by ensuring that you have the relevant personal protective equipment to enter the work area. Be mindful of the work activities taking place, if the environment contains lots of chemicals, dust or dirt you may not wish to wear your best suit!

As you enter the workspace look carefully in front, above, below, around and behind you to identify any potential hazards and familiarize yourself with the work area. Pay particular attention to warning signs and other local rules posted in the area.

## 3. Be strong

It's crucial that observers have confidence in their task and this is demonstrated appropriately with respect for those around them and their opinions. Observations aren't audits! Being strong is about being assertive rather than aggressive –remember the aim is to build relationships, foster agreement and drive improvement. So be direct about what you see, talk about specific issues, and use factual information. For example:

> *"I'm concerned to see that…*
> *There have been 6 near misses involving this in the last two months….*
> *What is the safe way to operate this…? "*

Remember that how we say things often has a more powerful effect than the words we use, so be aware of your body language. Aim for a relaxed, at-ease posture but don't slouch. Keep your hands free – don't fold your arms. Maintain eye contact when talking – look interested and avoid distractions.

## 4. Focus

Focus is everything. Use your plan to generate a clear picture of the outcome you intend for your observation. Pay attention to the way the discussion moves forward, and be sure to bring it back on track if it drifts off. Open questions can help bring out the real issues, but closed questions with 'yes' or 'no' answers can help keep things on course.

Don't jump right in. Begin with small(er) talk first, perhaps by showing a genuine interest in the person, asking about how long they have worked in the organization or department, the nature of the product that's being made on the line, how the job is done, etc. Then move on to discuss safety.

Your choice of questions is key here. On a recent observation visit as part of a coaching session with a senior leader I heard the following conversation:

Leader:    *"Hi, how's it going?"*

Worker:    *"Er, all good thanks"*

Leader:    *"Got any safety issues around here?"*

Worker:    *"No, everything's good"*

Leader:    *"Ah, great! Okay thanks, see you"*

This 'observation' lasted a total of 35 seconds. You can draw your own conclusions as to it's impact and success. After a coffee and some discussion with the leader I was delighted to observe her next attempt:

Leader:  *"Hi, this looks interesting. What are the main safety risks in this job?"*

Worker:  *"Well the moving machinery I suppose"*

Leader:  *"Can you explain why, I'm not an expert on this particular process"*

Worker:  *"Well the invert arm could come over and catch your hand if you're not careful"*

Leader:  *"Right, so the invert arm could injure your hand?"*

Worker:  "Yes"

Leader:  *"Oh, right. So how do you stay safe?"*

Worker:  *"We use this interrupt button to isolate the moving parts if we need to get into the machine, shall I show you?"*

This second dialogue continued for around five minutes, and culminated in a series of suggestions from the worker about how things could be improved. As we left the workplace, smiles were evident on the faces of both the leader and the worker.

## 5. Feedback

Following up on observation visits is vital. If during a conversation you identify and agree actions to be taken, gain agreement with the worker on specific things to be done, by them and by you. Be sure that the necessary time is taken to organize these and make a point of returning to the work location to share updates with those who have raised the issues with you. Think about how you can use the outcomes from your observations to share learnings more broadly across the organization, too.

In his handy little book *The One Minute Manager*, Ken Blanchard encourages us to *'catch the person doing something right'*. In conducting safety observations it's so easy to fall into the trap of doing the opposite though, and telling people what they've got wrong. With every observation, try to find a positive action to thank your colleague for. Not only will it break the ice, but it provides a great place to build further discussion from.

## Talk it up!

Below you'll find some phrases that can help you with your observations. Which others can you add to the list?

> *"If I were working alongside you today, what would I need to know to be able to work safely?"*
>
> *"What could you personally do to make your task here safer?"*
>
> *"What could I help you do that would make it safer around here?"*
>
> *"What support do you think your team needs to make things safer?"*

.................................................................................................................

.................................................................................................................

.................................................................................................................

.................................................................................................................

.................................................................................................................

.................................................................................................................

.................................................................................................................

# Performance

*'Good safety is good business'* is a common mantra. But how do we quantify the value that good safety performance brings?

A common method is to measure the number of accidents that occur. There have been many calculations done which tell us that each Lost Time Injury ('LTI') costs somewhere between $27,000[1] and $43,000[2] to the organization. So if we simply take the number of accidents that have occurred this year, compare that to last year's numbers, and then multiply the difference by the financial statistic of your choice we have something tangible to offer up…

> *Thirty fewer LTIs this year means we've saved almost $1.3 million.*

Fabulous! Well done! Really? Does past performance improvement come with a guarantee for future success? Of course not! The fact that we have not had any accidents for X days / weeks / months / years does not mean we are immune to them occurring today, tomorrow or ever again. Look at the trend data for accidents and injuries in your organization. I'm guessing that the curve looks something like this:

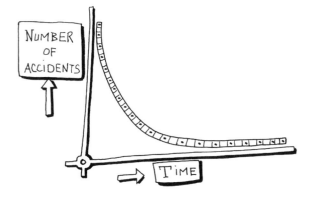

A while ago you enjoyed a period where you made great progress in reducing the number of accidents. Whilst you may have had some tough periods where there were a few 'spikes' in the number of accidents occurring, overall when you average it out, the curve continues on a downward trajectory, right? But right now, you're noticing that the curve seems to be flattening out.

You've got an *asymptotic curve.*

The word *asymptote* is derived from the Greek *asumptotos* which means '*not falling together*'. In simple terms the line of the asymptotic curve is getting close to the target (in your case this may be zero accidents) but not quite converging with it. This means things are slowing down. But you know this already. When you began your efforts in risk reduction you saw huge leaps forward in reducing accident numbers, then over time those sorts of reductions have been harder and harder to achieve, and now you tell yourself and your stakeholders that all the 'quick wins' have been taken, so naturally it's harder to gain further improvement. But actually what's happening here is that things are stopping working. <u>The effectiveness of your approach is reducing</u>.

Talking with my friend the great Sidney Dekker[3] this week we were discussing asymptotic curves. When I asked why he thought so many organizations used them fanatically he began "*well, the trouble with LGI charts is…*"

I gently whispered *"LTI"* as he spoke, but he seemed oblivious and carried on: *"so, yeah, LGI curves are really only good for the Boardroom and the senior execs…"*

I was in shock: this guru of the safety world didn't even understand one of the most commonly-used acronyms! I *had* to help my hero. Third time lucky. Taking a deep breath off, I went. But Sid took an even deeper breath and explained to me that '*LGI*' was precisely what he had meant to say. Dekker had created a new term: the LGI, or '*Looking Good Index*'. Same chart, same data, new name.

This new idea really got me thinking. It was true, all too often we measure our success in safety by the absence of stuff. The fewer negative events that occur, the better. Year after year we set targets like '*reduce the number of accidents by 20%.*' But this is crazy! Setting objectives for what we don't want to create pulls us away from managing the things that can actually create something positive.

Rather than measure what we value, we fall into the trap of valuing what we measure. We track accident numbers and offer the latest reduction as valid indicators of performance, but where else would it be permissible to measure the negative as proof of something positive? I would bet that your organization doesn't measure customer satisfaction by the fact that no-one has called to tell you that they don't like your product. We must measure what we do, not what we don't do. We must measure what we do to *create* safety.

*'But those charts showing LTI rates are a core element in our monthly safety reports to*

*the Board!'* I can hear you cry. Yes, I know, but are they adding any <u>value</u>?

I suggest that they don't. But your leaders *love* them, because it allows them to look good – and feel good. The charts build confidence that everything is moving in the right direction. How many times have you presented your LGI chart – sorry, LTI chart at the Board meeting and received sincere nods of approval and direction to *"Keep on doing what you're doing"*? Why does this happen? Well, Apollo Robbins, dubbed the 'Gentleman Thief' asserts that this is because as humans we have an inbuilt natural resistance towards straight edges. Robbins reveals that the technique at the heart of many of his slight-of-hand tricks is the *way* he moves his body. At risk of incurring the wrath of the Magic Circle he explains that people's eyes are more easily misdirected to follow a curve than a straight line. So despite the logic that a steeply reducing straight line might be a more direct route to accident reduction, our audience is predisposed to appreciating that curve!

So you leave the Boardroom scratching your head. You have a robust management system in place, good risk assessments, thorough accident investigations, everyone attends safety training. *'Okay'*, you think, *'we'll push a bit harder'*. But asking people to 'work more safely', or to 'try harder' just will not work. Doing more of the same thing will not lead to something different.

Despite the early wisdom of guys like Heinrich and Bird, there is literally stacks of research now that confirms there is limited predictive capability to be gained from data measuring the number of LTIs. Low numbers of LTIs does not mean that no fatal accidents will occur.

Safety performance needs to be measured against specific safety objectives, not the number of accidents that have occurred. Yes, I know that this book is called *From Accidents to Zero*. But think back to our Prologue: I explained that if we are to move closer to our vision of a workplace that is free from injury, we need to focus on **creating safety** rather than reducing the numbers. Attaining zero accidents is an <u>outcome</u> of what we do.

No matter where you are on the asymptotic curve, you can have a positive influence on safety <u>and</u> reduce the number of accidents in your workplace *right now* by changing your perspective and encouraging others to do the same. Make an effort to shift from measuring the negative – accident frequency rates (or 'lack of safety') towards measuring the positive (a safe workplace).

Make a mindset shift to accentuate the positive and eliminate the negative. Start by looking at the positive contributions being made to improve safety on a daily basis: team talks; sharing learnings from accidents; Lean Six Sigma projects; employee engagement; safety conversations; impactful training; workforce suggestions – there will be plenty to choose from. Consider how you can measure the impact of these. Think about useful leading indicators that can efficiently measure your *input* activities, that help you to be able to recognize and reward great efforts, to identify best practices, and to leverage improvements. Remember that achieving high levels of safety performance needs means and methods, not just the commitment and will.

## Measure what matters

1   How do you measure safety? Is that *'Days Since Last Accident'* sign by the employee entrance really encouraging good performance? Don't measure your success by the absence of negative events. Choose one or two measures that demonstrate the positive.

2   Think about how you discuss performance: move your language from *'Do we have any injuries?'* to *'Is it safe?'*

3   The Boardroom always enjoys good news. If the morale argument doesn't get their hearts racing, don't be afraid to talk hard cash. Protecting the bottom line and preventing accidents are not mutually exclusive. Talk positive: switch the conversation from 'reducing accidents' and reposition with the creation of safety in the workplace as an investment, rather than a cost. Speak about 'value proposition', 'return on investment' and 'early payback'. These little phrases will certainly grab attention.

## References

1   The International Labour Organization estimates each LTI to cost an organization 20,000 Euro or around 27,000 US Dollars.
2   National Safety Council and NIOSH in the United States of America.
3   Sidney Dekker is the author of many fantastic books on safety ay work. I highly recommend *The Field Guide to Understanding Human Error* for a fascinating insight into human behaviour and culture.

# Quality

Twenty years ago as a young engineer, my remit – alongside Safety, Health and the Environment – also included Quality. At that time there seemed to be a concerted effort to drive the four disciplines together into one framework. I was told that because each could be managed with systems and frameworks it made sense to save time, effort and resource to have them fall under the responsibility of one department. As a naïve youngster I nodded appreciatively and got on with my work, enjoying the mix of activities in which I became engaged and sucked up the opportunity to broaden my skills base.

Since that time, the trend for integration appears to have reversed and for many organizations the four strands have become separated back out into specialist functions. My own career has continued in a similar way; principally focusing on safety and risk, with others taking on the baton for quality. I've continued to observe strong synergies between the disciplines, however.

Just a few years ago, immediately following our most recent global financial crisis, I picked up a book that I thought might inspire some new thinking. Its title – *Out of the Crisis* – certainly resonated even though the book had been around a while. Written in 1982 by William Edwards Deming it argued that in order for organizations to succeed they needed only two things: commitment and an ability to open themselves up to new thinking.

Deming, considered by many as the '*father of Quality*', went on to articulate fourteen principles for management to follow in order to significantly transform both the quality and the effectiveness of their business. Let's have a look at them now:

1  Create constancy of purpose towards the improvement of products and services, with the aim to become competitive and to stay in business. Decide to whom top management is responsible
2  Adopt the new philosophy. We are in a new economic age. Management must awaken to the challenge, must learn their responsibilities, and take on leadership for change

3   Cease dependence on inspection to achieve quality. Eliminate the need for inspection on a mass basis by building quality into the product in the first place
4   End the practice of awarding business on the basis of price tag
5   Improve constantly and forever the system of production and service, to improve quality and productivity, and thus constantly decrease costs
6   Institute training on the job
7   Institute leadership. The aim of supervision should be to help people and machines and gadgets to do a better job
8   Drive out fear, so that everyone may work effectively for the company
9   Break down barriers between departments
10  Eliminate slogans, exhortations, and targets for the work force asking for zero defects and new levels of productivity. Such exhortations only create adversarial relationships
11  Eliminate work quotas on the factory floor. Eliminate management by numbers and numerical goals
12  Remove barriers that rob the hourly worker of his right to pride of workmanship
13  Institute a vigorous program of education and self-improvement
14  Put everybody in the company to work to accomplish the transformation. The transformation is everybody's job

As I read each of the points in turn, a bell rang loudly in my mind. The same is happening right now as I relay them here for you. Nearly a quarter of a century after they were proposed, I offer that Deming's principles are as relevant today as they were then. In fact, I'll go beyond that. Deming's principles are <u>more</u> relevant today than they were when they were originally published.

In a world where change is the new normal and business transformation is core to survival, these fourteen points offer a clear framework for success.

And what's more:

I think that Deming's fourteen principles also provide us with a robust roadmap for driving sustainable safety improvement in the workplace. It's fair to say that back in the '80s some critics slammed into the list for proposing a set of goals without providing the tools to reach them. In his classically empowering (if perhaps a little direct) Deming style he usually responded

> *"You're the manager, you go figure it out."*

## Let's figure it out

1   Review the list of the fourteen principles one more time. This time round, think of each one as referring explicitly to safety. How could you take each principle and turn it into a specific action for your workplace?

# Risk

Risk can have a serious impact on an organization, its people, and the communities in which it operates. How we identify and respond to risks will affect our performance, including safety aspects like our goal of reaching zero accidents. Our approach to risk will also affect how our organizations are viewed in the public eye. Effectively managing risk is therefore at the core of organizational success. It's also the cornerstone of our work in safety too.

Risk really means anything that prevents us from meeting our objectives. It can be typically broken down into three types:

**Operational** – ensuring day-to-day activities *(including safety)*
**Strategic** – the planning and decision-making processes
**Compliance** – meeting governance and regulatory obligations

In simple terms, risk is a function of three critical components: ***probability*** (of a particular event occurring), the ***severity*** (of the consequence of the event), and ***exposure*** (the opportunity of the event occurring). An easy way to express this is the formula:

*** Risk = Probability x Severity x Exposure ***

It's important to note that each of the elements function individually as well as multiplicatively. So if in our risk assessment we conclude that one of probability, severity, or exposure is zero, then overall the risk for that specific situation will disappear.

Assessing safety risks in the workplace can be a tough challenge. Their breadth is one aspect – from the natural to technological, from physical to psychological. But within these themes, scales of tolerability – typically ranked in numbers or from 'low' to high' – proliferate. With this wild diversity attempting to assess risks using one common approach is meaningless.

Before we go any further, let's be clear: this little chapter won't explain how to conduct a risk assessment. After all, if you've picked up this book I have a feeling you are already involved in assessing risks. Instead, we'll think about some of the issues that underpin effective risk management.

First, we must be mindful that when it comes to matters of risk, everything isn't black and white. Risk is all about *perception*. How probability, severity and exposure are viewed and assessed will depend upon the person's perspective and experience.

Within an organizational environment groups of individuals will naturally hold differing views on risk due to their own personal sensitivities. Some people may be concerned about practically all workplace hazards, whereas others may appear indifferent. This variation is caused by each individual's *cognitive* consideration of risk perception (the probability of an accident) and the *emotive* aspect (how worried or safe they feel when they think about a particular risk).

Most people are naturally biased when it comes to assessing risk. We use '*reference points*' anchored deep in our brains to compute the level of risk we believe we face. For example, one senior leader I work with views all forklift truck operations as 'very high risk'. It matters not to him that the drivers may be well trained, wearing seatbelts, and observing speed limits. Instead, his reference point is an event several years ago when one of his employees suffered a fatal accident involving a forklift. As the site manager at that time, this event resonated deeply within him and created such a deep anchor that he now views all forklift activity at the same level of risk.

A strong safety culture consists of <u>shared perceptions of risks</u> related to safety and its management. This is a crucial point, as the level of risk perceived in any given task has the potential to alter the approach and level of safety management applied to it.

In fact, perceptions of risk can negatively impact on the risk management process. Let's go back to the manager and the forklifts. His heightened sense of risk may at first be seen as a good thing, but over time it may come to be regarded as excessive by his peers. He continues with his focus and determination and validates his approach on the basis of there being no forklift accidents in his area of responsibility. Surely then his keenness is justified?

Hang on for a second here. We should be aware that there's a significant correlation between current accident rates and the perception of risk – both by workers and by leaders. Gradually reducing accident rates seem to foster a sense of comfort and confidence: as the numbers drop, so too does the perception of risk in the workplace. It's here we reach a tipping point, where confidence becomes over-confidence and leads to a false sense of security in the boardroom and encourages a perceived invincibility and short-cutting on the shop-floor.

But risk perception doesn't just operate in one direction. At the opposite end of the spectrum, I believe that there's a culture of fear growing within our societies that encourages people to overestimate risk. It's driven partly by the media who are seeking sensational headlines for television and newspapers and it's amplified by the actions of ordinary people who feel the need to wrap kids in cotton wool, remove hanging baskets of flowers from village high streets for fear of them falling on someone's head, and organizations stopping the weekly staff five-a-side football game in case an accident occurs.

This *'risk aversion'* is a concept based on the behaviour of humans when exposed to situations of uncertainty. In simple terms, a risk-averse individual, when given the choice between two options, will usually choose the one with the least risk. This dislike of risk, prompts individuals to choose what they perceive to be the safer option – even if this results in lower return. Now I can fully appreciate the right to choice, and in fact I endorse and support individuals making their own mind up about risk *(indeed my own personal hobbies and pastimes – free-flying, swimming with sharks, and rock climbing – all revolve around my own ability to take informed decisions about risk)* – but just for a moment imagine what an organization dominated by risk averse individuals might feel like…

So why is a culture of fear growing in organizations around the globe when it comes to matters of safety? I suspect that it's because we – the safety profession – have not sufficiently informed our leaders to allow them to be able to make appropriate decisions. [1]

This lack of information fuels extreme reactions. Either the over-confidence mentioned earlier, or risk aversion. When you train people to be risk-averse, you prepare the entire organization to be reward-challenged. Hold on, I'm not saying that we should encourage everyone to leap out of planes, swim with sharks or continuously take risk, but rather to *step forward and embrace risk*. Look it in the eye, understand it, and <u>then</u> take an informed decision on what to do next.

Maybe these extreme reactions are a result of the pressure felt by organizations around their reputation. Risk of course impacts the desire of customers to deal with an organization and *'reputational risk'* has become an area of fast-growing importance to all organizations as the process of globalization breaks down barriers to business and shrinks the commercial world considerably. An organization's reputation can be damaged by things as diverse as supply chain issues *(such as child labour involved in the production of clothing)*, ethical issues *(like bribery or corruption)*, and operational issues *(for example poor safety performance, fatal accidents, etc)*. Supply chain issues damaged the reputation of one of the world's biggest supermarkets recently, when horsemeat was found inside the store's brand of beef burgers and in other chilled meals. The ensuing result for Tesco was a sustained drop in chilled and frozen food sales, but also a more immediate impact: the corporation's share price was reported to suffer a blow which wiped out almost 300 million pounds of value.

Over the last century organizational attitudes to risk have undergone a seismic shift, thanks to deep research, myriad models and theories, regulatory concepts and major public events *(such as Deepwater Horizon, Rana Plaza in Bangladesh, Toyota car recalls, and many more)*. A change in the average corporate attitude – from risk aversion to a sense of balanced risk-taking – can thankfully begin to be observed in many commercial sectors. Despite this initial movement in attitude, and the apparent interest of senior leaders to take a more holistic view, there remains further opportunity for organizations to undertake a more strategic approach to managing risk in an integrated way.

Robust policies and procedures are essential if we are to embed risk management across the entire organization, though of course we must go beyond the formal frameworks and consider how we communicate on matters of risk. Risk Assessments, Matrices, and Registers are all helpful tools, but the most effective risk management systems will be the ones where everyone within the organization understands the risks in their operation, and what needs to be done to report, mitigate and control them. This is becoming known as *Enterprise Risk Management* ('ERM') where all risks are viewed together in a single coordinated framework as opposed to separate viewpoints for each risk type. Having safety integrated to an ERM framework[2] is good news for us as practitioners as it brings us closer to the heart of the organization's thought processes and decision-making and moves us away from the traditional view of safety as a 'bolt-on' or remote service provision.

Risk management – like our quest for zero accidents – is a continuous journey for every organization. Simplicity and clarity of approach are central to effective risk management and control. The answer is not more paperwork, but indeed more effective dialogue, conversation, and communication that allows our organization's leaders and workers to embrace risk and manage it appropriately.

## Step it up

1   What's the definition of risk in your organization? How does this definition (assumed or stated) influence the culture? Would you consider your organization to be at the tipping point of over-confidence, risk averse, or somewhere in between?

2   Is safety included in an integrated approach to risk management within your organization? If not, how could you align it with other enterprise risks?

# References

1  I'm generalizing here. I don't mean that it's all your fault, but I think that the 'collective we '– and I include myself here too – haven't always made it as easy as it could've been in the past. Do you?

2  If you're interested in a more strategic approach to enterprise risk management have a look at the ISO31000 standard. It provides a set of principles, a solid framework and clear process for the effective management of risk.

# Safety

What do you do for a living? Do you work in *safety*?

The chances are if you're reading this book, you're either working as a safety professional, on your path to becoming one, or you hold a special interest in the subject. Whichever it is, I'll bet you can answer the following question pretty quickly.

### *What is safety?*

Just for fun, and I know we might not get enough of that in this profession normally, go ahead and write down your definition here:

..................................................................................................................................

..................................................................................................................................

..................................................................................................................................

..................................................................................................................................

Now here's the rub. What you just wrote down is <u>not the same</u> as the other folks reading this book right now. And that's a big problem. Because each of you is working in a place where almost everyone else will have a variation on the definition that each of you have just written down. So here's another question for you. What does safety mean in your workplace? See if you can write that down here:

..................................................................................................................................

..................................................................................................................................

..................................................................................................................................

..................................................................................................................................

A little tougher? How do your two answers compare? Safety is one of those words that everyone recognizes and is able to define, but because we work in safety we perhaps overlook that our viewpoint may be different from those around us. Let's have a look at what safety means from a theoretical perspective by reviewing the utility of a couple of classic safety models, and then consider what it could look like in the future, if we just changed our perspective a little.

Back in the 1930s, our friend Herbert William Heinrich was a busy boy. Working for a large insurance company he had a stack of data at his fingertips. His 'discovery' of 'accident triangle ratios' certainly took the world by storm – and arguably still does.

Heinrich believed that 88% of all accidents were caused by the unsafe acts or behaviours of workers, 10% by unsafe physical conditions, and the remaining 2% through unpreventable 'Acts of God' [1]. He explained this through a series of linear relationships. To illustrate his point Heinrich presented his theory as a five factor accident sequence where an unplanned event or accident is caused by a succession of negative effects. The *Domino Theory* illustrates the process where failure of one factor actuates the next step, just like a line of dominoes being toppled consecutively.

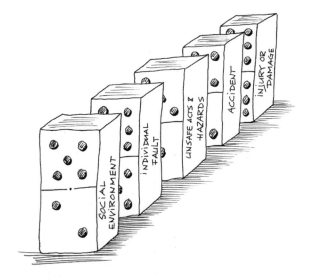

I can recall playing *Domino Rally* as a kid, lining up literally hundreds of dominoes around the house and setting off a chain reaction to knock the whole row down as it snaked around chair legs, *click-click-clicking* as it wound ever decreasing circles. I can also remember the way things would suddenly stop if just one domino was removed from the line. This in fact was Heinrich's premise – he argued that removal of just one of the factors would prevent the accident situation from occurring and the injury being sustained. Whilst scientific data was sadly lacking from his theory, it did provide us with a starting point to discussing how accidents occur. From today's perspective we've learned that things are a little more complex than toppling dominoes, but old Herbert did point the way towards the future: he suggested that the most important factor to be removed from the sequence was the one that stood third in line: '*Unsafe Acts & Hazards*'.

Taking Heinrich's third domino as a cue, we moved through the latter part of the twentieth century developing our understanding from treating safety as a hardware issue to realizing we needed to look at the software too. We began to first explore human factors, then looked into behaviours, and eventually organizational culture became *de rigueur*. James Reason picked up on this breadth of influencing factors and, through his famous *Swiss Cheese* theory of accident causation explained that whilst we can install several successive layers of defence – such as procedures, management decisions, barriers, training and other controls etc. (the cheese slices) – against workplace hazards, there are always flaws (the holes in the cheese) hidden within each layer which, when aligned, create a '*trajectory of accident opportunity*' where the hazard effectively passes through the holes aligned in each slice and causes an accident to occur.

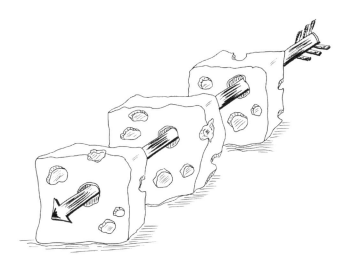

Reason's model suggests that the more weaknesses there are in a system (the holes in the cheese), the more chance there is of system breakdown leading to an accident (when the holes line up). The model has undoubtedly been highly influential and has shaped the accident investigation processes for many organizations around the globe.

Accident causation theories like the *Swiss Cheese* and the *Domino* model encourage us to gather data. We investigate what went wrong using *5 Why*, *Fault Tree* or *Fishbone* analyses to determine the primary, secondary and root causes which are then loaded into our databases and provide us with super lists of things we need to find and fix to put things right and stop the bad things from happening again. We tighten up our procedures, build better barriers, deliver more training, install improved lighting, replace broken parts, tell people to work safer. The trouble with this approach though, is that it works in retrospect. We use these models to identify where the holes have arisen, or how the dominoes have fallen <u>after</u> the event. Hindsight is a wonderful thing, but do we really need to wait for things to go wrong? Although his labelling may not be truly accurate, Heinrich certainly was on to something when he indicated that 2% of the causes of accidents were hard to pin down.

Whether our preference is for dominoes or cheese, the *causality credo* – as Erik Hollnagel calls it – prevails right around the world. The credo operates on the commonly-held belief that accidents happen *because* something goes wrong. Once we find out what ultimately went wrong (the 'root cause') we can fix it and thus prevent a repeat of the accident. The *Domino* and *Cheese* models have helped us to learn that consequences are preceded by causes but where the models lack is that they encourage us to assume that all causes can be identified. And that's just not the case in the real world, is it?

The other issue with following cause and effect models dogmatically is that we become preoccupied with 'finding and fixing'. It's simply impossible to ensure that things go *right* just by focusing on stopping things from going *wrong*. Counting holes in a slice of cheese may take things forward a little but it won't get us much closer to our goal of zero accidents in a safe workplace. The holes in the system will always be there. Just like when you slice into a lump of cheese, you just don't know when you're going to see them – or where they will align. Our systems, policies and procedures may look strong. We may feel proud of the solid training programmes we have put in place and refresh every year. Our risk assessments may be the best we've ever seen. But whether you believe it or not, sometimes, maybe just sometimes, what goes on out there on the shop-floor may not match exactly what it says in your procedures. So we can build our robust Safety Management Systems and then hope for the best, or we can try something different. What do you fancy?

My suggestion is twofold.

First, we look for the holes starting to appear. We can do this in one of two ways:

- Testing by functions not directing involved in the work activity – for example formal, structured safety audits or inter-departmental cross-audits can help to identify holes

- Independent assurance by an internal audit function with external experts brought in as required can provide an objective view and spot the smaller holes that may have been missed by departmental reviews

Second, in addition to our audits which are looking for the once-in-a-thousand things that go wrong, we get out there and look for the nine hundred and ninety-nine things that go <u>right</u> – and then encourage more of that.

So I urge you, let's please stop seeing *safety* as a reactive situation where we try to get as few things as possible going wrong.

Don't wait for the dominoes to fall, or the cheese holes to align before taking action. Let's take a new view and create a <u>proactive</u> definition of safety that means getting as many things as possible *to go right*.

Let's make a mindset shift from *preventing accidents* to *creating safety*.

## Slice it up

1   Look back at your definitions of safety at the beginning of this chapter. Did you or your peers consider that safety was a condition where the number of accidents was as low as possible? Did your definition include the notion of managing risks and eliminating hazards? What does this tell you about your culture?

2.   What could you do *right now* to start to make a mindset shift towards proactive creation of safety?

## References

1   These ratios have been debated for many years, the current prevailing view is that they are not accurate, with human behaviour now accounting for up to 95% of all accidents.

# Trust

As we've discussed elsewhere in this book, people are the key to developing a positive culture towards safety in your organization. DuPont, one of the world's leaders in workplace safety, advocates that building relationships that span and interconnect through all levels of the organization is a crucial factor when it comes to galvanizing corporate culture. Whilst the DuPont *Bradley Curve* [1] primarily charts the development of safety culture and the role it plays in reducing accidents, what the curve also underlines is the importance of growing and sustaining social relationships. As an organization moves from the 'dependent' phase to the 'interdependent' phase on the curve, it experiences a dynamic shift in the relationships between followers and leaders, and between peers. At the outset, workers in dependent organizations are characterized as following the rules because they *have* to, whereas those in the interdependent phase are typically following rules because they *want to*. At this point, workers take on the role of being *'each other's keeper'*: essentially looking out for, helping, and caring for each other to work safely. What lies at the heart of this change? Well, when we look deep into successful organizations – whether we're interested in safety, productivity, innovation or any other aspect – we observe that the most productive groups within them all exhibit high levels of interpersonal *trust*.

In 1988 Robert Levering wrote a book called *A Great Place to Work: What Makes Some Employers So Good (and Most so Bad)*. The book reflected interviews conducted with several hundred employees at companies all across the United States. Levering's assessment methodology became such a valuable tool that today annual listings of *'The Best 100 Companies to Work for'* are now produced in several countries around the world. I began to wonder what makes a company the best in the world to work for, so when I noticed the book was sitting at the back of my bookshelf I picked it up and opened a page at random. *Trust* leapt out at me. Levering was so convinced of the importance of trust that he lists it as the very first factor in defining a *Great Place to Work*.

The American political scientist Francis Fukuyama was equally convinced and cites concerns on whether team members can be trusted as one of the most powerful reasons for individuals resisting engaging in team-working opportunities [2].

The picture was becoming clear to me: if relationships are the lock, trust is the key.

So how do we develop trust in the workplace? Placing trust in another person is a social transaction directly related to the perceptions one has of a blend of attributes, notably:

- **Respect**: recognising personal worth and professional contributions of others

- **Fairness**: equitable sharing of opportunities and rewards

- **Honesty**: transparent sharing of information

- **Reliability**: consistently doing what you said you would do

- **Authenticity**: linked to honesty, authenticity is literally about being yourself [3]

- **Competence**: utilising the necessary skills to deliver effective performance

These attributes lie collectively at the core of *trustworthiness*. We demonstrate them through the words we use – both in their choice and through our intonation – and in the actions and behaviours we undertake. With a consistent approach to living these values we concurrently *give trust* to those around us, and *build trust* in our own social relationships.

Getting out into the business is paramount. Here's three ideas to help you build more trust into your relationships in the workplace:

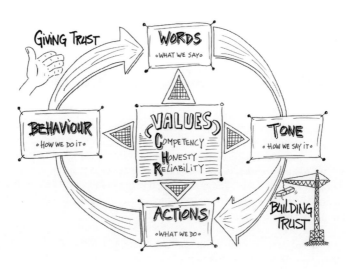

- Remember that no-one knows everything. Research shows that admitting that *you* don't know everything and asking questions to plug gaps in your knowledge can significantly increase the trust others place in you, without damaging the level of respect you've already build up. So ask questions, listen carefully, and repeat to check your understanding.

- In the *7 Habits of Highly Effective People* Stephen R Covey encourages us to *'catch a person doing something right.'* Whilst this may feel a little strange at first, the power of positive feedback in building trust is immense.

- Most people come to work to do a good job. Most people go home hoping that's what they've done. A sincerely said *'thank you'* might just be the two most powerful words you use today and strengthen a relationship more quickly than anything else you do.

To conclude, here's a very short course on trust, inspired by one of my personal leadership heroes, and arguably one of the world's greatest leaders, Sir John Adair, United Nations Chair of Strategic Leadership.

The seven most important words: *I am sorry, I did not understand*

The six most important words: *I admit I made a mistake*

The five most important words: *I am proud of you*

The four most important words: *What do you think?*

The three most important words: *Would you please…*

The two most important words: *Thank you*

The one most important word: *We*

The least important word: *I*

## Trust the process

1    Look back at the six attributes of trust. Which of these do you think you may be able to improve for yourself? What actions could you take right now?

2    In each of your conversations with your colleagues today, try to find an opportunity to offer a 'sincere thank you' for their contribution.

# References

1   http://www.dupont.com/products-and-services/consulting-services-process-technologies/
    operation-risk-management-consulting/uses-and-applications/bradley-curve.html
2   See Fukuyama's excellent book *Trust: The Social Virtues and Creation of Prosperity* if you're interested
    in more depth on this topic.
3   The word *authenticity* comes from *autos*, the Greek for '*self*' and hentes meaning '*being*'.

# Unsafe Acts

In this chapter let's do some real-time scientific research. Ready?

Gather together a group of people; somewhere between twenty and a hundred would be ideal. It doesn't matter if you know them all or not. It doesn't matter if they are male or female, young or old. Like the best studies, mix it up a little, keep it real.

Ask them all to stand. Then, ask them to sit down IF they read a statement on the screen which they have personally engaged in.

Here's what you'll have on the screen:

HAVE YOU EVER KNOWINGLY:

DRIVEN ABOVE THE SPEED LIMIT?
HAD UNPROTECTED SEX WITH SOMEONE YOU DID NOT KNOW WELL?
CONSUMED NON-PRESCRIPTION DRUGS OF ANY KIND?
USED A HAND-HELD TELEPHONE WHILST DRIVING?
PARTICIPATED IN AN 'EXTREME SPORT'?
DRIVING A MOTOR VEHICLE UNDER THE INFLUENCE OF ALCOHOL?
ATTEMPTED TO RIDE A WILD ANIMAL FOR A BET?

[You CAN ADD YOUR OWN ALTERNATIVES HERE TOO]

The chances are that within a few seconds of the slide being on your screen, most of the research group will have sat down.

So what did your little experiment prove? Well, it proves that almost everyone on the planet is capable of undertaking *unsafe acts*. Why is this so? The answer is remarkably simple: because we've been doing it <u>all of our lives</u>.

Since we were children, maybe even since babies, we've had the potential to be unsafe. In fact some of us even *deliberately* did it. As kids, when our parents tried to guide us into doing the right thing, to keep us safe from harm, we sometimes did the *exact* opposite of what they said. And we went further – we tried not to get caught.

We never liked being told that we 'have to' do something, so we rebelled. We wanted to do what <u>we *wanted*</u> to do. Hold this thought and quickly push the fast-forward button in your brain. Do you enjoy doing things now when you are told you 'have to' do them? Me neither.

Time for another experiment...

Reassemble your group of people and ask those who admitted to driving above the speed limit to identify themselves [1]. A hand in the air will do.

Now ask them *why* they drive above the limit. The majority will respond with something like *"It saves me time."* Okay, now ask them what speed they are typically doing on these occasions where they are driving beyond the limit. I'll bet you that the majority will say that they drive somewhere between five and nine miles per hour above the limit. Others may say 'up to ten percent over the limit'. Few, if any, will admit they regularly drive more than ten miles per hour / ten percent above the limit.

What's happening here is exactly the same as when we were kids: we still don't like being told what to do so we instinctively feel like *we* should be able to judge for ourselves what we do. We rebel by choosing our own speed limit to drive at.

We choose that fraction above the limit because psychologically we believe that we are back in control of what we are doing, and because ten miles an hour or ten percent above seems to be the magic number above which we believe there is a higher risk of 'being caught' [2].

Think back to the explanation your little scientific group just offered you:

**"It saves me <u>time</u>"**

Whether your group was comprised of senior executives, shop-floor workers, cool young things, relaxed retirees, or even safety folks, one thing unites them all.

Time.

Time is precious.

Time is money.

Time is life.

Time is one of the most persuasive factors when it comes to us undertaking unsafe acts. Even when we *know* that we're breaking the rules. Even when we *know* that those few extra miles-per-hour won't *really* get us there much faster.

Our desire to 'win time', especially when coupled with our human nature to dislike being told what to do is very powerful indeed.

'Winning time' is of course just one of the reasons behind why we have unsafe acts. James Reason, considered by many people to be one of the founding fathers of safety culture, suggests that unsafe acts are caused by a variety of factors, though he helpfully groups these into either *violations* or *errors*.

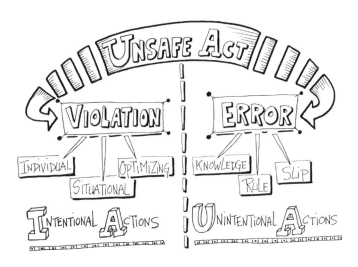

*Violations* are intentional actions taken either in response to or in anticipation of, something.

- *Individual* violations are deliberate, conscious decisions taken in direct response to a specific personal need – just like in our example of driving a car above the speed limit in order to 'win time'.

- *Situational* violations occur as a result of exposure to a particular situation prevailing at the time.

- *Optimizing* violations are typically undertaken with the idea that they will please others.

*Errors* are unintentional actions, or 'mistakes' that occur inadvertently and without the deliberate thought involved in *violations*.

- *Knowledge* based errors typically result from a lack of information or training.

- *Rule* based errors occur due to a gap or weakness in the system or rules governing a process or activity.

- *Slips* are temporary, fleeting failings which occur during the completion of a task or activity.

This model allows us to see that we need to consider both sides of the coin – looking at both intentional *violations* and unintentional *errors*.

When you dig into your unsafe acts (you could do this for your own personal acts, or on a grander scale, those within your organization) you'll likely find that many are unintentional *errors* catalyzed by the design of the workplace, a lack of training, work pressures, or personal factors such as tiredness.

Over on the flip side, when we analyse the drivers for the conscious behaviours that lead to *violations* we will see that beyond the time factor discussed earlier, a large proportion will be due to the individual believing that this was actually what was wanted or expected of them. An individual worker taking safety risks to get the job done, in the same way his colleagues do, in order to satisfy the supervisor's demands for production figures before the shift ends is a perfect example of how strongly persuasive these Individual, Situational and Optimizing factors can be.

## Time out

1   Thinking about workplace safety, choose an area where you've seen a recent trend for accidents, injuries or near misses. Ask workers if there is anything about their job that slows them down, or causes unnecessary drag. Instead of just telling them to work safely, find out how you can help them work more *efficiently* to achieve what they want to achieve at work each day.

2   Make a simple analysis of your recent accidents and near misses. What is the proportional split between *violations* and *errors*? What are the major trends

that you see in the data? Where should you focus your attention right now?

## References

1  If you are a police officer, this experiment may work better if you're not in uniform. Please remember it's just a fun little exercise not an opportunity to throw people in jail.

2  Yes, we could spend some time talking about perceptions here, but instead let's keep on track. We'll talk more about risk elsewhere in this book.  If you'd like to read some fascinating stuff on risk perception, do have a look at the work of Paul Slovic or Sidney Dekker.

# Values

In the chapter on *Culture* the word *values* popped up fourteen times. Now that's statistically significant in my view, and accordingly encourages us to consider things in a little more detail. In that chapter we introduced the notion that values shape an organization's culture and guide the behaviours of those who work within it.

Given that this book is all about culture, I'm going to suggest that rules-based safety only works for so long. Culture has a far stronger impact on behaviour. After all, when no one is around to enforce the rules – nightshift, weekends, or when the boss is on tea break – it's culture that influences what people do when backs are turned and no one is watching them.

Whether publicly advertised, articulated within internal vision statements, or woven into leadership dialogue, *values* are the principles or moral standards of an organization around which decisions are made and actions are taken. Values should enable the organization's beliefs to be upheld and effectively govern the behaviour of people. Earlier in this book Edgar Schein introduced us to the concept of *espoused values*. Whilst values in their own right can be difficult to see in isolation, they can be interpreted through observation of specific behaviours. Accordingly, the strength and influence of organizational values increases exponentially when they are *espoused* – or adopted and demonstrated – by senior leaders.

The values chosen to reflect an organization's beliefs are obviously going to vary between businesses, however there appears to be some degree of commonality. In a review of the values of one hundred multinational organizations, I found the following to occur frequently:

*Trust, open dialogue, constructive feedback, just culture, no blame, adaptability, collaboration, openness, research-based knowledge, pragmatism, common sense, innovation, safety, pragmatism, creativity, people first, zero harm, flexibility, can-do attitude, mindfulness, sustainability, agility, people first, equity, harmony, pride, camaraderie, quality, respect, accountability, engagement, empowerment.*

Which of these resonate with you?

Values can be seen as a kind of corporate 'culture compass' with which to navigate the blizzard of organizational complexity. As safety leaders, our stakeholders – no matter who they may be – will view us as more effective in our role when we bring a sense of clarity to our leadership philosophy and approach. In their book *The Leadership Challenge*, Jim Kouzes and Barry Posner reveal that where followers believe that their leader has a coherent set of values that guide their decisions and actions they become up to 40% more likely to engage in new activities in the workplace.

Beyond this initial engagement, research from the world of Human Resource Management confirms that where there is a close match between a person's values and those of the organization the commitment of that individual to the organization is stronger and longer lasting. These employees feel a stronger sense of pride in their work, and are more willing to put in extra effort because they feel like they 'fit'.

One of the challenges in achieving a robust safety culture is gaining agreement within the organization on how to implement and manage safety consistently in the workplace. Such an agreement clearly needs to include the buy-in and ongoing commitment of senior executives, the accountability of managers, and the active involvement of middle managers and supervisors. The question is, how do we go about this in something as complex as a modern organization?

Well, in recent years it's become popular for organizations to have a set of *safety values*, in addition to those at a broader corporate level. Whilst these are usually developed to suit the unique needs of each organization, examples of safety values might include:

- Safety is our first priority

- All accidents are preventable

- Safety is a condition of employment

- We are all responsible for safety

- Everyone has the right to say STOP for safety

- We all work in safety

- We operate a just culture with regard to safety

- All incidents, accidents and near misses are reported and investigated

Setting out our organizational beliefs around safety through clear values statements offers the benefit of being able to 'lay out our stall' and send a message to the workforce that safety is important and *of value* to the business. Articulating clear safety values also allows for the creation of specific actions, linked to particular values, which can then be observed and measured as part of a performance improvement programme.

But we must be mindful of a potential – and very significant – pitfall here…

Safety needs to be embedded in the DNA of a company so that it becomes 'how we do things around here' (remember our simple definition of culture from earlier in this book?). To make this happen we need to 'walk the talk'.

Look back to that list of safety values. Did you notice the first one? It's not really a *value* is it? Many organizations seem to fall into the trap of declaring that '*safety is number one*' but then through their actions – at leadership level, right down through managers and supervisors – they demonstrate that this just isn't the case. As a result, people begin to quickly realize that it's not a value at all: it's just PR spin.

Allow me to share recent experience. I was on a walkabout in a factory belonging to a large global manufacturing company. Arriving on site I was ushered to a small room and given a safety induction. When I asked what was the most important thing to know about the way the company worked, the site manager proudly explained that *Safety First!* was their motto, and that safety *always* took priority over productivity, profit and any other issue. As we stepped onto the shop-floor I noticed a number of posters repeating the slogan. I couldn't help but feel the majority looked a little worn and tired around the edges. Some had suffered tears and rips in the hustle and bustle of working life. Occasionally '*Kilroy*' popped up just to let us know that he '*was 'ere'*. In the middle of the factory was a large banner suspended from the ceiling. Emblazoned across it was the phase

### *SAFETY FIRST at (Name of Company)*

The banner had clearly been up there a while: the rope holding the top right corner had worked loose and one edge had slipped down making it hard to read. The thick black dust from the industrial processes below had obscured some of the wording and dulled the once-vibrant colours. Leaving the factory, our tour continued into the yard area. Just next to the employee entrance was a large noticeboard, the left hand side of which had been reserved '**For Safety Notices Only**'. There was the corporate *Safety First!* poster, looking a little faded from the sunshine, and pinned over its surface were several smaller notices: '*Car for Sale*'; '*Babysitter Available*'; and one looking for players for the company's next five-a-side football game. The safety message was almost obliterated from view. We made our way back to the boardroom and as we climbed the stairs I was surprised (though perhaps I shouldn't have been) to see a sign declaring… *Quality First!*

As we began our debriefing session, the manager was clearly oblivious to what I had seen. Each example I offered was met with disbelief. The banner *'must just have slipped today'*; the noticeboard adverts had *'likely gone up last night'*; the quality sign was probably the quality department *'having some fun at the expense of safety'.*

Later, when we were joined by a group of shop-floor workers, we asked for their views on safety. The consensus quickly became clear: that safety *"used to be* important" but *"nowadays it seems to be just one of a bunch of things we need to try to get done before the bell rings at the end of the day".*

The guys from the frontline were able to demonstrate, more ably than I, that safety had clearly slipped in the list of priorities for the company. It was not viewed as one of the core values of the business at all, and the demonstration of leadership commitment – in allowing the banner and posters to become obscured – reinforced this message to the workforce.

The company's efforts to espouse safety as one of their values had backfired. By positioning it as a *priority* they were doomed to failure. Safety <u>cannot</u> be the number one priority for any organization. The top priority for every business must surely be to generate sufficient sustainable profits and cash flow to satisfy stakeholders and maintain business operations. There will be other priorities too: delivering a specific order, maintaining a certain standard of quality, hitting a sales target, achieving *Investors In People* status. The list goes on and on. When we try to add safety to the list, it becomes *one of* the priorities. And as we all know, priorities change. When safety is seen by employees to slide down the list, it sends a powerful message indeed.

Positioning safety as a value allows it to share *equal importance* with the handful of things that really matter to your company. The things that are not subject to climatic influence like order book pressures, staff availability or cost of materials. That's not to say that our values don't change. In a humourous but extremely insightful study, Dan Gilbert and his partners found that as individuals our values change over time. In early adulthood (between the ages of 18-28) the research reveals that we consider *pleasure* as a core value to pursue. By the time we reach middle age, it's all about *success*. And in our later years we turn to *honesty* as being the most important. In a similar way it is to be expected that our organizational values may change too. Taking the time to occasionally review and revise what's dear to the corporate heart generates terrific opportunities to refresh our communications and remind everyone about what's important and why.

For our 'corporate culture compass' to work effectively and help our colleagues navigate efficiently every day, we as leaders need to be in constant communication with the workforce to show how their contributions connect to the organization's values. So, for example, if one of our corporate values is *'we always work in safety'*, then a key question you might ask of colleagues could be *'how does your role ensure we all work safely today?'* Even the flashiest of posters and catchiest slogans on banners can't compete with that.

## Connect the dots

1   Choose three of the values that guide your organization. Now consider how you connect your work in safety to these values. Are you aligned?

2   Do you think safety is positioned as a priority or a value in your organization? How do the workforce view it?

# Words

Chances are, if you're reading this book you're either accountable for leading an organization; responsible for managing, directing or advising on workplace health, safety and / or risk management; studying safety or a related discipline; or, if none of the others apply, you may be simply working in an organization with other people around you. Whichever one it is, you'll likely find yourself in a position where you communicate with others.

Beyond the simple good manners of polite communication, if you work in an organization that employs people, you'll <u>need</u> to communicate with people to exchange views and ideas, and to issue and receive instructions. There are, of course, myriad benefits of getting workplace communication right: employees feel more involved and empowered, leading to improved morale and wellbeing, higher productivity, and increased efficiency. In short, good communication is good business sense, and arguably, critical to organizational success.

Research [1] indicates that human factors are a primary cause in around 80% of all workplace accidents and one of the principal issues in the disasters of Bhopal, NASA's Challenger, the Piper Alpha oilrig explosion, the nuclear disaster at Chernobyl, and the recent BP events. So surely it makes sense to talk with those around us about how to prevent injuries and improve safety at work? The feelings of connectivity and personal engagement you create within your colleagues, co-workers and peers will build into demonstrations of advocacy, and create a stronger momentum that you can on your own.

With 180,976 words in current circulation within the English language [2], we certainly have plenty to choose from when constructing our communications. But talking about safety is not quite straightforward. How people perceive and understand words like *risk, hazards, danger, compliance* and indeed *safety* can vary considerably and these perceptions may be sufficient to cause concern or lead to confusion and misunderstanding. Even with just a cursory surf through my dictionaries I can find no less than 14 synonyms for *safety*, and a further 37 for the word *safe*...

Workers receive hundreds of messages each day – and our safety communications compete with all of them. If we want to be sure that our messages will land on target we need to be mindful of what else is going on out there.

Imagine you've just arrived at work and you're logging into your computer system. The little welcome sound pings in your ear and you're ready to begin. You open your email inbox and watch as the screen fills with a sea of red unanswered emails that have arrived since the last time you were online. What do you do? Do you take each one in the turn that they arrived on your computer, paying each your undivided attention until it's resolved or answered?

No, you look for *keywords*. Perhaps for you, words like *urgent, priority, emergency, accident*, or the name of *your boss* all command your immediate attention. Just like the way we scan, ignore, delete and react to our emails, our safety communications are treated similarly in the workplace. Of course we could try sticking keywords like *urgent* onto our messages and see if that works, but I suspect it may get a little dull over time. Instead let's shift our gaze to beyond our own world for a moment.

Some time ago, Yale University undertook a study to identify the most powerful and persuasive words in the English language.

Here they are, in reverse order:

10  New
9   Save
8   Safety
7   Proven
6   Love
5   Discover
4   Guarantee
3   Health
2   Results

It's interesting to note that the eighth most powerful word in the world is *safety* isn't it? It's always been popular, though. In the 1976 cult classic movie *Marathon Man* the lead character's catch-line appears to be *'Is it safe?'* as he fears for his every next step. Society today remains fascinated with *safety*: we demand safety from everything in our lives – from the products we eat, to the cars we drive, the financial investments we make, our children's toys – but I can't help but wonder if we've lost the meaning of the word. In the recent horsemeat scandal in the United Kingdom [3] one supermarket proudly proclaimed *"Our burgers are 100% safe to eat"*. Really? Is this *good* news? Shouldn't all of the food products from your store be 'safe to eat'? Using the word in this way can propel our minds towards negativity, so let's be careful with its usage.

I've been fascinated with the way the word *safety* draws so many negative connotations. Often the mere mention of the word is enough to bring a change in conversational direction, glum faces, or downright disgust. Here's a quick example. I was at a dinner party recently when the person next to me asked what I did for a living. I began to explain that I worked in safety. No sooner had the magic word left my mouth, my inquisitor responded by telling me that the weather forecast for the weekend looked exceptionally good, and then promptly asked whether I intended to be outside doing sports or such like.

So with several experiences like this I've been thinking about the language we use when we talk about our work. From the outset I've been wondering what we might call safety if we had the opportunity to redesign our language? Would it be *integrity*? Organizational risk? Or *reliability*? What would you choose?

An interesting little project known as the *One Word Interview* works in a similar way to provoke our thinking. Thought leaders, shapers and influencers from around the world are asked for their views on workplace safety (for example, the value of safety, challenges and big issues) in the present and also in the future. Each person is asked just five questions. Sounds like an easy enough interview, but the sting is in the tail – each answer can only be one word. The One Word Interview directs us to distil our message and focus our attention on what matters most. Have a look at www.onewordinterview.com or www.onewordonsafety.com to learn more about this groundbreaking idea and see if you can take the challenge to reduce your focus to <u>just one word.</u>

In this age of information it's easy to ignore the challenges of communication. It's even easier to use words that we feel are 'normal' to us when we talk about safety in the workplace. But how much of what we say is jargon, overly-technical, or difficult to decipher abbreviation? Whilst a discussion of *Generations X and Y*; the differences between *now and then; them and us*; and the times that *went before* us is beyond this chapter, wherever you are, and whatever you're doing, it's vital to understand your target audience and their communication preferences. Consider demographics, psychographics, cultures and prevailing attitudes fully and then adjust the content of your communication, your style, your words and your delivery methods accordingly.

As we close this chapter, whether we are in times of organizational change or a period of relative stability, building and delivering clear, concise and consistent safety communications that resonate with our target audience is vitally important. Getting this right will enhance the credibility of workplace safety and help demonstrate the human skills that lie at the heart of safety leadership.

To shift perceptions positively I respectfully suggest that we start with ourselves. Let's think about what we are really here for. First I propose that we need to move from being *advisors* (*the ones who 'tell'*) and *practitioners* (*the ones who 'do'*), to being *enablers* (*the ones who 'make things happen'*).

Then we need to review our vocabulary and choose *words* that *grab attention, encourage engagement, influence behaviour* and *make an impact.* Courageous conversations are required if we are to help our stakeholders *discover* a *new* way of doing *safety* they can *love*, and that *guarantees results*.

Who can do this?

*You* can do this. After all, *you* are the most powerful word in the world[4].

## Let's talk

1   Review the most recent safety communication or campaign in your workplace. Can you easily identify the key messages? How have keywords been selected to create an impact?

2   Ask a selection of colleagues, workers or peers what the key message was in the latest safety campaign. Which words do they remember? Why?

## References

1   Health & Safety Executive, 2009.
2   The Oxford English Dictionary, 2nd Edition, lists 171,476 words in current use, plus an additional 9,500 derivatives also in common parlance.  There wasn't enough room in this chapter to list them all.
3   Where horsemeat was found within products marked as 100% beef.
4   Right at the top of the Yale study was the word you; the most persuasive word in the entire English language.

# X Factor

In around 430b.c. Xenophon was born in Athens. He went on to become a soldier, and a historian, though he is remembered more easily as a student of Socrates. Although Xenophon was not regarded as one of the classical Greek philosophers his writings have shaped much of the modern day science of leadership.

In some of his more considered annotations, Xenophon pares down the art of leadership and reveals the importance of building culture:

> *"The true test of a leader is whether his followers will adhere to his cause from their own volition, enduring the most arduous hardships without being forced to do so, and remaining steadfast in the moments of greatest peril."*

How does Xenophon propose we go about this?

> *"The first duty is to sacrifice to the gods and pray them to grant you the thoughts, words and deeds likely to render your command most pleasing."*

The idea of sacrifice is certainly beyond the realms of this book – and perhaps even a little *avant garde* for many of today's methods of modern management, but in praying to the gods, perhaps what Xenophon is seeking here is the *X Factor*. That unknown element or inexplicable thing that adds a certain value or strong influence. It's that certain *je ne sais quoi*.

In our pursuit of safety excellence, we've come to learn that effective leadership is about going beyond technical knowledge, organizing skills and a compliance focus in order to develop a sense of maturity that takes us from the 'management of things' and allows us to gain an understanding of people, their behaviour, motivation and influence. But is there also *'something-you-can't-quite-put-your-finger-on'*? What's the *X Factor* that ties it all together?

Socrates would tell Xenophon that *"Wisdom begins in wonder."* So if we were to pray to the gods of safety, what *X Factor* wisdom might they bestow upon us in order to make our approach *'most pleasing'*? Here's what I think they might offer their students now:

## The X Factor – 15 Divine Elements

**Acceptance of Ambiguity** – Embraces the diversity of the workplace and takes a proportionate approach to managing risk, as opposed to blindly pursuing total risk elimination

**Learning Culture** – Sufficient emotional intelligence to understand that people are fallible and accepts genuine mistakes as part of the learning process and not punished automatically

**Action Visualization** – Sees the steps needed along the journey, as opposed to achievement of the destination

**Big Picture Perspective**– Avoids getting stuck in narrow mindsets, sees with a wide-angle lens and articulates how safety fits, aligns with, and supports the broader business aims and objectives

**Language Fluency** – As the great Nelson Mandela said *"Speak to a man in a language he understands and it goes to his head. Speak to him in his language and it goes straight to his heart"*

**Flexibility** – Understands that black and white thinking rarely delivers constructive progress and more often that not eliminates options. Operates with the purpose of providing service for others

**Agility** – Ability to select multiple options to progress and move swiftly to execution

**Tolerance of Complexity** – Acceptance and understanding that everything isn't simple but able to find the sweet spot or balance point in each situation. In the words of French singer–songwriter French Alain Bashung: *"Si tout est compliqué, ça ne colle pas, si tout est simple, ça ne suffit pas"*. Bashung's line translates as *"If everything is complicated, it doesn't work. If everything's easy, its not enough."*

**Gratitude Attitude** – Consistently acknowledges the worth and contribution of each individual in an appropriate manner

**Horizon Awareness** – Continuously scans the horizon and makes sense of new ideas, theories and discourse, introducing these to the cultural melting pot

**Constructive Curiosity** – Able to critically challenge the status quo – whether systems, procedures, policies or cultural aspects – by contributing disconcerting questions constructively and with respect

**Drive and Perseverance** – The ability to self-motivate, set appropriate goals and manage our time efficiently. Come hell or high water showing up every day and getting the job done well

**Optimistic Influence** – Inspiring and motivating positive action in others towards their goals

**Confident Independence** – Not depending upon systems and hierarchies, craving acceptance and surrounding themselves with head-nodders and yes-men. Prepared to be seen to be different and secure in one's own right

**Nonconformity** – Ability to see beyond mere conformance (compliance) and move past 'checklist-thinking'

## Beginning to wonder

1   What's the *X Factor* that makes safety come alive in your workplace? Is there a certain something that pulls everything together?

2   Which of the *15 Divine Elements* do you feel are the most important? What steps could you take to introduce these to your organization?

# You

Yes, *you*.

I don't mean anyone else; I really do mean just *you*.

*You* are all is this chapter is about.

*You* are the reason that I wrote this book.

*You* have read these chapters with interest, objectivity and attention.

*You* have listened to my thoughts and developed better ones of your own.

*You* have generated great new ideas.

*You* can lead change.

*You* are the one they listen to.

*You* are the one they're counting on.

*You* are the one they're waiting for.

*You* can make a difference.

*You* are the one that makes all the difference.

*You* just have to decide where to begin.

The momentum that *you* create will be hard to resist.

Thank *you*.

## It's all about *you*

1   Take a full five minutes just to think about *you*.

2   Identify your own personal strengths – how can you leverage them now to create more safety in the workplace?

3   What about your weaknesses – where are the opportunities for personal growth?

4   What are you passionate about? Are you pursuing this as you would like to?

5   Make a list that has two actions for each of the three previous points

# Zero

It's everywhere isn't it?

Last week I noticed a *Zero Tolerance for Verbal Abuse* sign in the airport.

At the station I read about the train operator's commitment to *zero harmful emissions*.

Arriving in downtown New York I visited *Ground Zero*, before meeting a nutrition-fanatic friend for lunch. She chose *zero fat* salad dressing on her *zero calorie* kale salad. I chose a high-octane steak though opted for a *zero sugar* cola drink to balance the calorie count. The sauce may have been light but it sure left some heavy stains on my shirt. When the hotel laundry service sent it back to my room after cleaning I noticed some damage that I was sure wasn't there before. Calling reception I'm advised of the hotel's *zero liability policy* and told I'd sent the shirt at my own risk.

Today, when my motorbike coughed and spluttered, I flicked through a magazine and felt seduced by the latest offering from *Zero Motorcycles:* a 100% electric motorbike featuring *zero maintenance, zero oil, zero gas, zero exhaust fumes.* My bank, acknowledging the tough economic climate, generously offered me a *zero percent interest loan* [1] that would help me buy it with *zero delay.* I decide that I'll stick with the bike I have, and drop the magazine in recycling. Committed to *zero waste* in my house.

Over in the UK, a new Government *zero carbon* policy requires all new homes built from 2016 to mitigate emissions produced on-site. Whilst next door to my home in Switzerland the construction site advertises that all their new apartments come with a *Zero Defects Guarantee.*

By now I'm realizing that it's everywhere I go, but I'm guessing that you, dear reader, place *zero* weight on these anecdotal observations so I decide to check with the fount of all knowledge. Unsurprisingly I get over 262 million *(that's six zeros by the way)* hits for the word *'zero'* on Google. Feeling frazzled, I reach for a drink, but as it's late in the evening I choose the *zero caffeine* option, a nice herbal tea.

We've taken *zero* on whole-heartedly in our profession too, haven't we? Hands up who has a target of *Zero Injuries? Zero Accidents? Zero Harm?*

The great English poet John Donne remarked about zero:

> *"The less anything is, the less we know...*
> *How invisible, unintelligible a thing is zero."*

The word *zero* comes from the Italian *zefiro* which itself is derived from the Arabic *safira* meaning 'empty' or 'nothingness'. But even after tracing its origins, Donne was right: zero is elusive. Achieving zero is a serious challenge. Try it for yourself: try *doing* zero <u>right now</u>.

Goals and targets of zero do not appear anywhere else in our world. Why? <u>Because they simply do not motivate us to act</u>. Whether in industry, sport, personal development, parenting, education or health, we just don't set zero goals because we understand that framing progress *in terms of loss* is demotivating. No matter who we are or what we do, we are more interested in *gaining* something of value, than thinking about what we might lose.

The language and discourse around zero is disruptive too. The problem with zero is that it's an absolute: there is no room for manoeuvre, nowhere to go, no tolerance. It stands in sharp contrast to the notion of continuous improvement that forms the bedrock of quality assurance, environmental best practice and so many more disciplines that share synergy with safety. The intolerance that we project when we say we want zero injuries (or zero harm, or zero accidents) feels rather elitist. Do we really intend to apply this zero tolerance across all aspects of our organizations? Will we have zero tolerance for the mistakes of managers, men and machines in the workplace?

Social psychologist Dr. Robert Long suggests that:

> *"The language of zero only inspires perfect people. The rest of us are motivated by patience, tolerance, understanding and the scope to learn and mature."*[2]

As Dr. Long points out, the real outcome from an organizational focus on absolute zero is a culture of confusion. Safety evangelists replete with branded caps, hi-visibility vests and waving flags and banners proclaiming *'Zero is my Hero'* strive to prevent every single paper cut, quell coffee spills, and have us holding handrails as we descend the two steps to the car park. Whilst at face value all looks well as the numbers steadily decline towards that big round O, if we care to turn our microscopes onto what's really happening inside the organization we find cynicism and skepticism have taken hold. Will we *really* stop production when a

Near Miss is reported? What happens when a minor accident occurs? Does that sticking plaster make the event an 'injury' that resets our day-counter back to… *zero*? Each time it does, we must surely reset our expectations along with the clocks. How many resets before we really lose track of what time it really is?

Look, I understand that talking about zero is attractive. It's easy. People *'get it'*. It feels right. It looks good. But as a *goal* or *target* it is, quite frankly nonsensical. Now before you jump to the natural conclusion and accuse me of wanting or accepting accidents if I don't have a goal of zero, let me just offer that there is no room for such binary opposition when it comes to safety.

Binary opposition is where things are explained through the use of two mutually opposing terms. Think of a light switch – it goes off, or on, right? When it's off, it's certainly not on. And vice versa. The central premise of binary opposition is simple: if it's not one, it's the other. There's no 'in between'. So binary oppositionists think that if you don't believe in God, you must believe in the devil. If you don't support the 'war on terror', then you must be a terrorist. Could it really be true that if you don't have a goal of zero injuries, then you must endorse harm??? [3]

In this short chapter we are restricted by space, so whilst our discussion could run for much longer, we must work to curtail it now. If zero is our goal perhaps you may think that's fine – after all, what other number of accidents and injuries should we choose to accept and aspire to? But this dedicated focus on zero as the goal is risky, because it:

- Builds a culture of intolerance

- Increases a fear of failure

- Drives reporting underground – or worse, fosters a climate of deceit

- Diverts attention away from the big picture to focus in on microscopic risks

- Crushes creativity

- Engenders a reactive mindset

- Focuses on failure

- Shifts us from effective risk management to pedantic risk elimination

- Stifles openness, transparency and trust

- Kills flexibility

- Reflects the past, rather than looking to the future

- Revolves around naivety

- Distorts our data

- Promotes penalty and punishment

The list above could go on. It's true that when it comes to workplace safety we all *hope* that no-one will be killed or injured on the job. In fact we strive for it every day. But hopes and aspirations are like dreams – hard to quantify and difficult to materialize. Attaching a number doesn't make it any easier.

The ideology of zero is a distraction from the main game, as people end up so in love with counting numbers they forget about humans.
For years we've learned that goals must be S.M.A.R.T[4]. At some point we'll have to stop and ask ourselves whether a goal of zero really is.

## Reset the counter

0.1 How does your organization talk about risk? Consider the language and communication media utilized – do you think that your organization promotes a culture of learning and tolerance, or one of absolutes and reactivity?

0.2 How could you provide a *value gain* to motivate people in safety?

0.3 I suggest that whilst we can *commit* to zero, we should strive for <u>safety excellence</u>. What does excellence look like to you? How would you recognize it in workplace safety?

## References

1    Subject to status. Terms and conditions apply. Your home may be at risk if you make zero instalments to repay your loan.
2    Long, R., 2012.
3    Dr. Robert Long examines the discourse of zero from a risk perspective in his excellent book *For the Love of Zero*. I highly recommend it to you. Visit www.humandymensions.com.
4    The acronym S.M.A.R.T. typically stands for Specific, Measurable, Achievable, Realistic, Time-bound though are several variants around.

# Epilogue

So here we are at the end of our journey together. Let's pause for a moment to review where we came from.

We began this book with the aim of demystifing organizational safety culture. I suggested that if we switch our mindset (and our activity focus) from *'preventing accidents'* to *'creating safety'* we could achieve several beneficial outputs, including the sense of clarity needed to move through that cultural mist and drive a performance step change that takes us closer to our vision of zero accidents.

The overarching premise of this book has been that safety leadership is not a hierarchical duty but in fact a role that falls to each and every one of us, no matter who we are, or where we stand in the corporate structure. Along the way we've discussed various elements that make up what we refer to as safety culture including beliefs, values, behaviours, leadership and much more. After reading this book I hope you'll agree that improving the culture of safety in an organization is neither an onerous nor a necessarily difficult task. It begins with us getting out there and being proactive: with a pragmatic, proportionate approach to managing risks, a degree of mindfulness, and a range of 'soft skills' with those around us to build positive change that has significant and sustainable impact.

As you have worked through each of the chapters you've been presented with ideas, suggestions and proposals for action. Which of these resonated with you? Flick back through the book and choose just one thing right now. Choose one thing that you've read in this book that you think – given where you are with safety right now in your organization – will make a difference.

I wish you the best of success on your own journey *From Accidents to Zero* in whichever organization you work for. Remember that *every* journey, no matter the distance or destination, begins with a single step. So choose yours and begin, today. Please let me know how you get on. Keep *creating* safety!

**www.fromaccidentstozero.com**

# References & Further Reading

This book has been designed to avoid lengthy academic references in our discussion. However as we've explored safety culture from many angles there have been mentions of several papers and pieces of research which you may be inclined to follow up in more detail.

In addition to these references, you will also find suggestions for your own further reading here.

Adair, J. (2010) *Strategic Leadership*. London: Kogan Page.

Blanchard, K. & Johnson, S. (2003) *The One Minute Manager*, New York: William Morrow.

Bregman, P. (2011) *18 Minutes: Find your Focus. Master Distraction and Get the Right Things Done*. London: Orion.

Buckingham, M. (1999) *First Break All The Rules*. Simon & Schuster: London.

Callaghan, G. (2002) Faith, *Madness and Spontaneous Human Combustion*. St Martins: New York.

Chabris C. & Simons, D. (2011) *The Invisible Gorilla: and other ways our intuition deceives us*. Harper Collins: New York.

Cohen, G. A. (2013). *Finding Oneself in the Other*. Princeton University Press: Oxford.

Covey, S.(1998) *The 7 Habits of Highly Effective People*. New York: St Martin's Griffin

Cox, S & Flin, R. (1998) *Safety Culture: Philosopher's Stone or Man of Straw?* Work and Stress (12), 3, pp189-201.

Darwin, C. (1859) *On the Origin of Species*. London: John Murray.

Dekker, S. (2008) *The Field Guide to Understanding Human Error*. Farnham: Ashgate.

Dekker, S. (2007) *Just Culture*. Farnham: Ashgate.

Deming, W.E. (1982) *Out of the Crisis*, Cambridge: Cambridge University Press.

Douglas, M. & Wildavsky, A. (1982) *Risk and Culture*. University of California Press: Berkeley.

Flin, R., Mearns, K., O'Connor, P. & Bryden, R. (2000) *Measuring Safety Climate: Identifying the Common Features*. Safety Science (34), 1-3, pp177-193.

Fukuyama, F. (1996) *Trust: The Social Virtues and Creation of Prosperity*. New York: Free Press.

Furedi, F. (2002) *The Culture of Fear*. Continuum: London.

Gardner, D. (2008) *Risk: The Science and Politics of Fear*. Virgin Books: London.

Geller, S. (2001) *The Psychology of Safety Handbook*. Lewis Publishers: London.

Giddens, A. (1991) *Modernity and Self-Identity*. Cambridge: Polity Press.

Gladwell, M. (2002) *The Tipping Point: How Little Things Can Make a Big Difference* Little, Brown & Co: Boston.

Gladwell, M. (2005) *The Tipping Point*. London: Penguin.

Glendon A.I. & Stanton, N.A. (2000) *Perspectives on Safety Culture*. Safety Science 34, pp193-214.

Goldstein, N.J., Martin, S.J. & Cialdini, R.B. (2007) *Yes! The Power of Persuasion*. Profile: London.

Grosz, S. (2013) *The Examined Life*. London: Chatto & Windus.

Hale, A.R. (2000) *Culture's Confusions*. Safety Science 34, pp1-14.

Hanh, T.H. (1991) *The Miracle of Mindfulness*. London: Random House.

Health & Safety Executive (2010) AALS Inspector Guidance Note – IGN 1.08

Health & Safety Executive (2009) *Reducing Error and influencing behaviour HSG48*. Sudbury: HSE Books.

Heinrich, H.W. (1931) *Industrial Accident Prevention: A Scientific Approach.* New York: McGraw-Hill.

Herrero, L. (2008) *Viral Change.* MeetingMinds: London.

Hofstede, G. (2002) *Exploring Culture: Exercises, Stories and Synthetic Cultures*

Hollnagel, E (2014) *Safety-I and Safety-II.* Farnham: Ashgate.

Hopkins, A. (2012) *Disastrous Decisions: The Human and Organizational Causes of the Gulf of Mexico Blowout.* Melbourne: CCH.

Kahneman, D. & Tversky, A. (2000). *Choices, Values and Frames.* Cambridge University Press: London.

Kahneman, D. (2011) *Thinking, Fast and Slow.* London: Penguin.

Klein, G. (2003) *The Power of Intuition.* Doubleday: New York.

Klein, G. (2011) *Streetlights and Shadows.* Cambridge MA: MIT Press.

Komaki, J., Collins, R.L. & Penn, P. (1978) *The role of performance antecedents and consequences in work motivation.* Journal of Applied Psychology, Vol 67(3), Jun 1982, 334-340.

Kouzes, J. & Pozner, B. (2008) *The Leadership Challenge.* San Francisco: Jossey Bass.

Levering, R. (1988) *A Great Place to Work.* New York: Random House.

Long, R. (2012) Risk Makes Sense. Scotoma Press: Australia.

Long, R. (2012) *For the Love of Zero.* Scotoma Press: Australia.

Lupton, D. (1999) *Risk.* Routledge: Abingdon.

Mack, A & Rock, I. (1992) *Inattentional Blindness.* Cambridge MA: MIT Press.

Marsh, T. (2013) *Talking Safety.* Gower: Farnham.

Marsh, T. (2014) *Total Safety Culture.* Manchester: Ryder Marsh.

Quilley, A. (2006) *The Emperor has no Hard Hat.* Safety Results: Sherwood Park.

Quilley, A. (2010) *Creating and Maintaining a Practical-Based Safety Culture.* Safety Results: Sherwood Park.

Quoidbach, J., Gilbert, D.T., & Wilson, T.D. (2013) *The End of History Illusion*, Science, 339, pp96-98.

Reason, J. (1997) *Managing the Risks of Organizational Accidents*. London: Ashgate.

Reason, J. (2008) *The Human Contribution*. Farnham: Ashgate.

Reber, A.S. (1995) *The Penguin Dictionary of Psychology*. London: Penguin Books.

Pressfield, S. (2002) *The War of Art*. New York: Black Irish.

Schein, E.H. (2004) *Organizational Culture and Leadership*. San Francisco: Jossey Bass.

Schwartz, T (2010) *The Way We're Working Isn't Working*. Simon & Schuster: London.

Slovic, P. (2000) *The Perception of Risk*. Earthscan: London.

Slovic, P. (2010) *The Feeling of Risk: New Perspectives on Risk Perception*. Earthscan: London.

Taleb, N. (2007) *The Black Swan: The impact of the highly improbable*. Random House: London.

Taylor, J.B. (2010) *Safety Culture: Assessing and Changing the Behaviour of Organisations*. Farnham: Gower.

Thaler, R.H. & Sunstein, C.R. (2009) *Nudge*. London: Penguin.

Townsend, A. S. (2013) *Safety Can't Be Measured*. Farnham: Gower.

Turner, B.A. & Pidgeon, N. (1997) *Man-Made Disasters*. Oxford: Butterworth-Heinemann.

Weick, K. (1979) *The Social Psychology of Organizing*. McGraw Hill: New York.

Wheatley, M.J. & Kellner-Rogers, M. (1996) *A Simpler Way*. San Franciso: Berret-Koehler.

Wiseman, R. (2009) *59 Seconds: Think a Little, Change a Lot*. Macmillan: London.

# Acknowledgements

It's been said that writing is a lonely endeavor. Fortunately that's not really been my experience. Although my name is on the front this book is covered by the fingerprints of many and I am sincerely grateful for them all.

Whilst it's impossible to mention everyone, there are several that need to be formally recognized for the impact that they've had on this process. Although he struggles to get his head around writer's block and the challenge of constant re-writes I thank my father for giving me his work ethic. Edwin and Juanita thanks guys for your awesome creativity; KP for never-ending positive vibes; Chet for that first push; AD for patient proof-reading; NMB for being a genius; V pour ta compréhension and Jeb for reminding me to take time out occasionally.

I am fortunate to have some of the sharpest minds in safety, culture, and risk management in my network and although you're scattered around the globe, your thinking continues to inspire and affect me on a daily basis. Thank you.

To my employers of the past: thanks for giving me the space to develop my thoughts and shape our approaches together, we've covered many miles on our various journeys to zero accidents. A special mention is deserved for those who have worked for and with me – thank you for your insight, your enthusiasm, and especially your collaboration. I always say that safety is a team game, and I've loved being on your team.

Thank you to my clients for engaging me to work with you and allowing me to share in your quest for safety excellence. I am grateful for the trust you place in me and take delight in *creating safety* with you.

Last but certainly not least, thanks to YOU for buying and reading this book. I sincerely hope you've found something of use within its pages.

# About the Author

**Andrew Sharman** holds masters degrees in international health and safety law, and in organizational behaviour. He revels in the interplay between compliance and culture.

With a safety career spanning almost two decades he has guided global leaders in their commitment to zero accidents and towards safety excellence across a range of industry sectors including power generation and supply, fast moving consumer goods, heavy engineering, and manufacturing. His experience spans more than one hundred countries across five continents.

Andrew has a reputation as a thoughtful, innovative, engaging orator and speaks extensively on the subjects of risk management, safety culture, leadership and organizational behaviour with corporations, NGOs and at universities. He has chaired or given keynote papers at more than one hundred professional development events around the world including the prestigious TED conferences.

Andrew is the Chief Executive Officer of RMS – international consultants on safety leadership and cultural excellence to a wide range of blue-chip corporates and non-government organizations globally, learn more at **www.RMSswitzerland.com**

Far from being risk averse, Andrews loves high risk adventure sports including free-flying, rock climbing, sea kayaking and swimming with sharks. He uses these pursuits to think differently about the language, perceptions and function of occupational safety, health, risk management and sustainability and to align these disciplines with broader organizational issues to drive positive impact and enhance the performance of individuals, teams and businesses.

Contact Andrew at **andrew@RMSswitzerland.com**

# Ordering Extra Copies

To order extra copies of **From Accidents to Zero** please visit the website at **www.accidentstozero.com**. Personalized inscriptions may be available upon request.

For bulk orders please contact at **info@fromaccidentstozero.com** for more information on discounts and shipping costs.

**Customized special editions** of this book can be created for particular audiences, such as a specific organization or event. A bespoke foreword from your organizational leader and a tailor-made introduction written by the author may be added. The cover of special editions may also be adapted.

You can engage the author in a variety of ways, from speaking opportunities to consulting services to support your own journey **From Accidents to Zero**. Just drop us a note at **info@fromaccidentstozero.com** to discuss.

I'd love to hear your thoughts on this book and your own journey **From Accidents to Zero.** Please drop me a line at **info@fromaccidentstozero.com** or **@ads_sharman** or **@RMarshSharman** on *Twitter*.

Looking forward to continuing the conversation!

# Books and Courses

## Safety Savvy

### What You Need to Know to Stay Alive Longer in a Dangerous and Uncertain World

The pressure to be safe and healthy is stronger now than it's ever been. The response to this is usually more policies, more procedures and more checklists. But is this really the answer?

Ideally suited for your entire workforce, **Safety Savvy** provides a refreshing antidote to the rules-based bureaucracy and with contributions from Brad Pitt, Tom Cruise, Nelson Mandela, Dirty Harry and Rocky Balboa this little book shares the five truths of the **Safety Savvy** in a way that will change your view of safety forever. Andrew Sharman and Tim Marsh strip back the bureaucracy to expose what really matters when it comes to personal safety – whether at work, at home, or at play – and using their trademark style of blending humour with hard facts leaves readers in no doubt as to what's necessary to live longer – and happier - in a dangerous and uncertain world.

*"This book takes famous movie quotes and cleverly relates them to situations in society which have an impact on health and safety, giving it a really broad appeal. Fits snugly inside your back pocket - ideal to pull out when sitting on the bus, waiting for a train or just relaxing down the pub. In fact, it's written in a style that feels like the authors are chatting to you over a pint, asking you, the reader, the questions, making it highly thought-provoking."* **SHP magazine**

*"Simply brilliant! Buy copies for all of your team."* **Graham Redpath, Emtelle**

Visit www.maverickeaglepress.com and enter code FATZ20 for **20% discount** on your copy.

# Mind Your Own Business

## What Your MBA *Should* Have Taught You About Workplace Health & Safety

For many leaders safety has become about paperwork, policies and procedures – doing things because others say they must be done, rather than doing the right thing and leading from the front. People can have very different ideas and understanding about risk in general, about how to identify which risks really matter, and how they can be managed effectively. This panoply of views makes it difficult for leaders to gain clarity and confidence about how they can play their true part in leading safety. So it gets put in the "difficult" box and leaders look to others to do it for them.

Together Andrew Sharman and Judith Hackitt get under the skin of how and why many leaders tend to complicate matters by compartmentalising different types of risk. They explore why leaders encourage specialists to take control for them and consider why responsibility for health and safety is delegated to others when leaders would not surrender other aspects of leading their business.

*Mind your own business* draws a line in the sand for 'stealth and safety' and argues that all leaders – no matter their prescribed remit or domain – need to embrace workplace safety in order to be successful. The book sets out to reframe health and safety as a core value and a real leadership mission. Sharman and Hackitt argue that a straightforward and inclusive approach to safety should be a core part of all management and leadership training – especially MBAs – and explains in clear, practical terms why and how, when it comes to matters of workplace safety, minding your own business will help you get things ***just right***.

*"Managers feel baffled by the complexity of OHS systems and regulations. What this book says will come as a breath of fresh air to them. There are so many myths to be debunked; importantly, managers really do not need to let fear of most unlikely legal consequences be a key driver of their decisions*

*Given the background and credibility of the authors, managers should see this as a strong signal to look again with confidence at their leadership in safety."* **Professor Andrew Hopkins,** sociologist and best-selling author of *'Learning from High-Reliability Organisations'*, *'Failure to Learn'* and *'Safety, Culture and Risk'*.

Visit www.maverickeaglepress.com and enter code FATZ20 for **20% discount** on your copy.

# Total Safety Leadership

The ***Total Safety Leadership program*** is a two-day masterclass for operational leaders and managers who want to make a difference in the way they lead with safety and forward-focused safety practitioners who are ready to think differently.

Based on the global best-selling book on safety culture ***From Accidents to Zero*** this masterclass is dynamic, fast-paced and highly interactive as participants explore key aspects of workplace culture from employee engagement and motivation, to risk-taking behaviour, affective communication and high-impact leadership.

***Total Safety Leadership*** is approved by the **International Institute of Risk and Safety Management.** Participants receive an IIRSM certificate on completion of the program.

Thousands of leaders from around the world have used the program to dramatically shift performance, improve culture and enable excellence in their organizations. Here's what they have to say about it:

*"Bright ideas delivered in a simple, straight-forward way, so that they went straight to our heads and to our hearts. We all know that rules and procedures are very important to build a robust safety culture, but Total Safety Leadership makes it clear that we also need to pay great attention to what people think and feel about safety. This program has significantly influenced my personal leadership style, in this regard let me express my gratitude to you once again."* **Chief Executive Officer, Oil & Gas industry**

*"An inspiring masterclass - the most impactful safety event I ever attended and now I have a zillion ideas on what I want to do differently to improve safety culture in my business."* **Global Director, Chemicals industry**

*"An fantastic program that really got me thinking about how I lead safety at work. The interactive approach brought several 'a-ha!' moments for me."*
**Operations Director, Automotive industry**

*"The energy in this program is contagious and the approach defies convention, breathing new life into what can be perceived as dry subject matter. Excellent!"*
**Department Head, FMCG industry**

Email **info@fromaccidentstozero.com** to find out more about running the ***Total Safety Leadership*** program in your organization.

# The Missing MBA Safety Module

You understand that the future of workplace safety is one where great leaders think differently and focus personally on engagement, empowerment and collaboration. And you know that this future starts *now*. But *how* do you get started?

The ***Mind Your Own Business MBA Safety Module*** is an inspiring, action-focused program for modern leaders striving to regain a sense of balance when it comes to workplace health and safety and fill that gap for those who have already completed their MBA program.

Building on the concepts in this book, you'll learn tools and techniques that will help you get the balance *just right* for your organization and create a ***Personal Leadership Plan*** to *mind your own business* and lead your organization to success.

The three-day program will help you to:

- Explore the culture in your own organization and understand the factors that *really* drive that culture
- Identify what's currently getting in the way of performance improvement, cultural maturity, and your leadership
- Envision a new future where safety and success go hand-in-hand and the balance is *just right*
- Build confidence in your ability to be an authentic safety leader
- Identify the *real* 'movers and shakers' in your organization who can support you on the journey – and those who might be holding you back
- Develop an action plan to deliver sustainable results in the new paradigm

This program is delivered exclusively by Andrew Sharman and Judith Hackitt through face-to-face workshops in small groups and individual one-to-one coaching, as the authors act as your personal guides and mentors to help you lead and manage safety efficiently, effectively and with impact whilst building shared accountability and measurable improvement both in health and safety performance and organizational culture.

Don't put it off! If this book has inspired you to lead on safety, email us now at **info@fromaccidentstozero.com** to find out more about working with Andrew and Judith on the ***Mind Your Own Business*** program in your organization, now.